JERICHO

Also by Charles Bowden

Killing the Hidden Waters (1977)

Street Signs Chicago: Neighborhood and Other Illusions of Big-City Life, with Lewis Kreinberg and Richard Younker (1981)

Blue Desert (1986)

Frog Mountain Blues, with Jack W. Dykinga (1987)

Trust Me: Charles Keating and the Missing Billions, with Michael Binstein (1988)

Mezcal (1988)

Red Line (1989)

Desierto: Memories of the Future (1991)

The Sonoran Desert, with Jack W. Dykinga (1992)

The Secret Forest, with Jack W. Dykinga and Paul S. Martin (1993)

Blood Orchid: An Unnatural History of America (1995)

Chihuahua: Pictures From the Edge, with Virgil Hancock (1996)

Stone Canyons of the Colorado Plateau, with Jack W. Dykinga (1996)

Juárez: The Laboratory of our Future, with Noam Chomsky, Eduardo Galeano, and Julián Cardona (1998)

Eugene Richards, with Eugene Richards (2001)

Down by the River: Drugs, Money, Murder, and Family (2002)

Blues for Cannibals: The Notes from Underground (2002)

A Shadow in the City: Confessions of an Undercover Drug Warrior (2005)

Inferno, with Michael P. Berman (2006)

Exodus/Éxodo, with Julián Cardona (2008)

Some of the Dead Are Still Breathing: Living in the Future (2009)

Trinity, with Michael P. Berman (2009)

Murder City: Ciudad Juárez and the Global Economy's New Killing Fields, with Julián Cardona (2010)

Dreamland: The Way Out of Juárez, with Alice Leora Briggs (2010)

The Charles Bowden Reader, edited by Erin Almeranti and Mary Martha Miles (2010)

El Sicario: The Autobiography of a Mexican Assassin, with Molly Molloy (2011)

The Red Caddy: Into the Unknown with Edward Abbey (2018)

Dakotah: The Return of the Future (2019)

JERICHO

Charles Bowden

FOREWORD BY
CHARLES D'AMBROSIO

University of Texas Press
Austin

Lannan
CHARLES BOWDEN PUBLISHING PROJECT

Copyright © 2020 by Charles Bowden
The Charles Clyde Bowden Literary Trust
Mary Martha Miles, Trustee
Foreword copyright © 2020 by Charles D'Ambrosio
Printed in the United States of America
First edition, 2020

Requests for permission to reproduce material from this work should
be sent to:
Permissions
University of Texas Press
P.O. Box 7819
Austin, TX 78713-7819
utpress.utexas.edu/rp-form

⊗ The paper used in this book meets the minimum requirements of
ANSI/NISO Z39.48-1992 (R1997) (Permanence of Paper).

Library of Congress Cataloging-in-Publication Data

Names: Bowden, Charles, 1945-2014, author.
Title: Jericho / Charles Bowden ; foreword by Charles D'Ambrosio.
Description: First edition. | Austin : University of Texas Press,
2020. | Includes bibliographical references.
Identifiers: LCCN 2019045001 (print) | LCCN 2019045002 (ebook)
  ISBN 978-1-4773-2095-2 (cloth)
  ISBN 978-1-4773-2096-9 (library ebook)
  ISBN 978-1-4773-2097-6 (non-library ebook)
Subjects: LCSH: Drug traffic—Mexico. | Cartels—Mexico. | Organized
crime—Mexico. | Narco-terrorism—Mexico.
Classification: LCC HV5840.M4 B69 2020 (print) | LCC HV5840.M4
(ebook) | DDC 364.1/33650972—dc23
LC record available at https://lccn.loc.gov/2019045001
LC ebook record available at https://lccn.loc.gov/2019045002

doi:10.7560/320952

Foreword

CHARLES D'AMBROSIO

I am dreaming.

It should be no surprise that death has something to say in *Jericho*, visiting the work with a voice of its own, but it's a death and a voice that have nothing to do with the slaughter on our southern border, nothing to do with the body count in Ciudad Juárez or the sicario and their ongoing tally of torture and murder, nothing to do with that whole vast army of the dead and the dying who for decades marched through nearly all of Charles Bowden's heroic work. The death that finally came for Bowden was his own, and it's that solitary death whose anguished and eloquent voice we hear calling to us in this somewhat—what? What is *Jericho*, exactly? I balk at calling it a book, if only because this morning the word leads my mind astray, up a stairwell into the musty and forlorn stacks on the fifth floor of some library somewhere, all that dying erudition on shelves no one visits anymore. So if not a book, what? Forget the codex, what's the actual experience, I mean as an act of discernment, an attempt to see and say what is *actually* there? Because death had its day, *Jericho* still carries in its pages the vitality of a draft, the secret ardor of the messy desk at a certain hour, of the coffee cup and the ashtray and the warm glow of a solitary lamp, offering the reader intimate access to the mind of the maker in the agony of getting it down. The glimpse we get in *Jericho* is privileged. It's not that we intrude on a man's privacy, but we do play the part of bystanders in his drama, now watching as fragments are fitted in place and patterns form, now shuffling a stack of images and tilting them to the light for a better view, now reading though a sheaf of crumpled notes in which every half-thought and dim hope get a resounding *stet* only because time ran out. There's a raw live edge to the accretion that gives the work a yearning, an ongoingness even though its author is gone, with *Jericho* caught now and forever in a state of desire, struggling to find a form.

It's not work meant for the easy chair, for the room at home where the lamplight is just so, the tea just so, the quiet just so. Any work whose mouth is full of fragments asks for a different kind of reader, one who'll dip a shoulder and join in a difficult labor, who'll divvy up the load with alacrity, accepting the burden and even taking on the heavier share. No essay or poem or novel can say what it needs to say alone, but in *Jericho* a kind of halfness reaches out, possibly for a reader, maybe for the touch of a helping hand, likely for something far more elusive. A hungry ghost seems to hover over these pages, but I didn't know Charles Bowden (Chuck to those who did). In the misguided belief that knowing the man might clear up a question or two, I read half a dozen of Bowden's obituaries, but only sank deeper into the riddle. He's got the same meager bundle of biographical facts we all do, but people seem to identify with the man as much as the work. Between the lines, of course, you hear the low hum of hagiography, of a saint in the making, one of those dirty saints with the cigs, the booze, the women. I suppose if Bowden hadn't written a shelf of nonfiction whose fierce ambition is unequaled in American (not so) *belles-lettres* we'd call him a barfly and be done with it. But he did write those books, books that are all one, continuous as a dream, laying out a tragic vision that's so noble and so singularly dedicated in its will to truth that it feels sacrificial. But before getting into all that, a curious fact from the obits did catch my eye, that Bowden walked out in the middle of the defense of his doctoral dissertation, ditching on the whole deal. This would certainly suggest a man who had the willingness and nerve to work without a net. Who does that? And don't we love him, instantly? In giving up pedigree you also forgo easy passage, perhaps for a lifetime, and at the height of the sixties, when demonstrations and protests were social, Bowden's was the boycott of a man who would go it alone. *Never a normal life for me.* By the early seventies he'd bailed on academe entirely, and to my knowledge never taught again. Truly a free lance all his days, a condition he described in a bio for an early book as "a free ticket to the asylum."

These days the civic art of rhetoric plays out in arenas a little less august than in Cicero's time, but our citizenship is still as powerfully shaped by rhythm and sound as it was in the heyday of the Roman Senate. With Charles Bowden you have to go to the likes of Abraham Lincoln or Woody Guthrie or Kendrick Lamar to find people who make as cool of a beat out of what is otherwise public discourse. Put the matter of Guthrie's "Hard Traveling" or Lamar's "DNA." in the mouth of a politician or social worker or professor or anyone you believe is in the business of persuasion and the appeal will likely come off as dull, preachy, obvious, ordinary, forgettable. A singalong might fare a little better, particularly in the case of Guthrie, but rote recitation wouldn't work at all, and in either case, I doubt we'd ask for an encore. Stripped of its music even the truth doesn't sound all that true, as the ancients knew. The truth of sound seems to travel on a lower frequency than sense and it's those unheard melodies that endear soul to soul. Crucially, sound is where art enters nonfiction, where discourse that aspires to the condition of art makes its claim to something more than ephemera, becoming news that stays news, as Ezra Pound put it. It also distinguishes art from the article, and the editors at the *Tucson Citizen* must have heard the truth in Bowden's early pieces or they wouldn't have printed such ghastly material in a daily paper. *I can only get started writing if I think it is music—that way I beat back my own cowardice.* Often a poet or essayist will own a pet word or two, taking the language private, inflecting it for his own expressive needs, and "coward" seems to belong to Bowden in much the same way "wicked" belongs to James Baldwin. He has something specific in mind, but it's hard to say what, exactly. By all accounts, including his own, Bowden led a bold and reckless life, full of audacious moves, and his field research exposed him to constant levels of risk that, unrelieved, likely kept a staggering volume of cortisol flowing to his brain. His was a life that exhibited a certain amount of fortitude, it would seem. A further complication here is that Bowden's talking about writing, about sitting at a desk and putting words on a piece of paper, not the sort of inconstancies, the derelictions and abandonments, more commonly associated with cowardice. That music is brave when we're not is hardly a case that needs making, not for anyone familiar with the military cadence or the spiritual or the sea shanty, but the writer is quietly alone in his work, not marching in formation or calling across a field or shouting at sea. It's possible that the writer alone at his desk is less alone in the company of a voice, and maybe that mix of rhythm and sound, the solace of a soloist, is a way of playing in unison, no different than a gang of gandy dancers mauling spikes to the beat of a railroad chant—the once-familiar voice of manual labor in America, before machines took over the jobs and silenced work songs everywhere but in prisons. The trick for Bowden, it seems, was to make a music that would carry the entranced writer past the objecting mind, which makes cowards of us all, and take him and his work and the reader into places none of them would otherwise go.

And where exactly was that forbidding place? I imagine Bowden rewrote like the devil—that's just an educated guess—but the fiddling had to be about something more than arranging facts or mounting arguments. It reveals a concern for another order of understanding entirely. There are hard-boiled beauties in all of his books, phrases cut like gems, moral insights made to last and hand down as heirlooms from a forgotten time. Or often his sentences mimic the mood of a ruminating mind, running on, blurred at the edges, a wall of sound that comes to us in the comma splices of a man who can't stop thinking. Or he seems to find a wary present tense expressive, but then the tone will switch up, withdrawing into a privacy, dwelling. *I was at some other place with my dead*. And remembering. *I still think of my dead, of all those women and children left slaughtered at the hands of strangers. They have stayed with me since my time covering crime for a daily newspaper. I still live in the same town and for me, it is studded with kill sites—lonely desert trees where a child's bones were finally found, alleys where dawn found a woman naked and cold and cut to hell*. Bowden's prose doesn't linger at the mirror, doesn't stop to primp and pretty itself in a passing window, but it isn't unaware of itself either. It's worked and reworked and worked some more and when that rhythm is finally right you know he's signed his name to every syllable. Why would he care though, why care so passionately about something others would consider ancillary to the presentation of facts, at most a frill, a fussy ornament, a pretention? Or simply a nuisance, standing in the way of a report's utilitarian purpose? Art prose always wants to make the world visible, to render what's unseen into a reality that's shared, but Bowden's sentences go a step further, it seems to me, doing the work of incantation, calling the dead back to life, and in the rhythm of those recalled moments you're right there beside him, breathing as he breathes, seeing what he sees, knowing what he knows. You're no longer reading a piece of reportage so much as standing in the presence of the original. There you are, in the lonely desert where the child's bones are finally found. There you are, in the alley where dawn finds the woman naked and cold and cut to hell. Now you've seen and that seeing implicates you. Now you're a witness and walking away is a moral peril.

The self who speaks to us is no less a thing of art. He's a Western figure, stark that way, either tough or tender, whose despairs are of the silent type and tend to suffuse the work rather than settle on the person. Along the way we might learn that Bowden stands 6'4" tall or that he doesn't wear a watch or that he fished with a cane pole as a boy on the family farm in Illinois. But mainly we don't indulge a biographical self so much as get a vision, a sense of the gaze, of a man standing his ground and staring (at his own destruction?) without the flinch that would lose the game. I'd characterize the vision as a keen vagueness, or a kind of readiness, alert to the unseen menace in the room, where the true subject is always on the periphery, out on the edge, in shadows, as if Bowden were always wondering: has something in the corner been left in the corner, overlooked? The voice that lifts this vision off the page tends to be dead serious in tone, a quality I admire as much for what it is—the very sound of solidarity and resistance—as for what it isn't, the easy-get of an irony whose corrosions, sayeth Kierkegaard, dissolve everything in a solution of doubt.

The art, the vision, the voice are all of a piece, a single fluent gesture, but facility of expression shouldn't lead us to assume that his subject matter was somehow fated too. Is a writer's true subject ever an *a priori* affair? Subjects that seem synonymous with Bowden are worthy now, in retrospect, and from a safe distance, but inevitability would seem to be in our eye alone. *The characters will not be grand enough, they never are . . . they are brown . . . they are the poor carving new lives out of the hungers and lies. . . .* Where would such a thing actually begin? Out of what nothing, in what quiet chamber of the heart? My guess is that the initial encounter was with an emptiness, an emptiness with an ylem of suspicion, a hinky feeling, a faint whisper in a whirl of noise, fragile as all infant things are. The first violence had to be raw, an insult to the eye, and the cruelties unspeakable, without pattern or meaning, vision or voice. *No one on earth wants this story.* For the artist, of course, no subject is inherently worthy or unworthy, in no small part because that way leads to propaganda, not art, with coercions that come from outside the work and call not for readers but for puppets. The writer has angels of his own and rises to them only through the action of his art. For me, though, the stubborn question remains, why all this difficult business, why the art, the vision, the wearying chase, when sturdy reporting and a simple byline would do? When accuracy and a fidelity to verified facts would still earn a paycheck? What was he after, finally?

Up on the fifth floor of that library somewhere, tucked in with all that dying erudition, you'll find a slender book by the German philosopher Karl Jaspers. It's called *Tragedy Is Not Enough*, and in it there's a brief discussion of Hamlet. The essential observation to make about Prince Hamlet is that he knows what no one else knows, and yet he's not sure that he knows it. There's the matter of that ghost.... *You can know some things and the knowing seems to help you not at all.* Jaspers says that any man in Hamlet's position begins to see all the world in a different light. "He keeps to himself what he can't communicate." *I make a note. But I have no idea why I make a note. There is no place to publish such a detail. I am not even certain I care about such details.* Every human being and every situation "stands revealed as in itself untrue through its resistance to the search, its subservience to a conspiracy against the truth. There is a flaw in everything. Even the best-intended among the good fail in their own way." *Nothing really helps. That is what I am trying to say. Theories don't help, therapies don't help, knowing doesn't help.* For Jaspers, the tragic occurs whenever awareness exceeds power, and by that measure alone Bowden would seem to have spent the better part of his life in a condition of helplessness, bound up, that is, in the tragic. *I am a coward. I am tired of the killing. I am pointless. I look but do not act. I listen and write things down and my words change nothing.* Jaspers goes on to describe the tragic condition and its atmosphere as a "strange and sinister fate to which we have been abandoned. There is something alien that threatens us, something we cannot escape. Wherever we go, whatever we see, whatever we hear, there is something in the air which will destroy us, no matter what we do or wish."

With the simplicity of a child, tragedy poses its questions to the world. What is true? Can truth be found? Who is right? Is the right cause ever successful in this world? Does truth conquer? *How do you live a moral life in a culture of death?* Those stark questions are the tragic figure's only possession, his uncorrupted will to truth.

But let's imagine life this way: say it's 1603, say a young Chuck Bowden goes to the Globe Theater, say earlier in the day he'd watched a chained bear disembowel a dog but now he's up near the stage, in a muddy pit, jostling with all the other groundlings who've paid a penny each for a performance of what, it turns out, is the premier of a new play. It's called *The Tragical History of Hamlet, Prince of Denmark*. It's Act 3, Scene 1. The famous soliloquy. (Now a brief aside: too often Hamlet's condition is dismissed as neurotic waffling, a surfeit of thinking and reflection that's supposedly the bad trait of dreamy boys, feckless in their intensity and outsized hopes, choking on possibilities, with no outlet in action. It's just a phase, the world counsels. But the world is

Polonius, smug in its truisms, encased in clichés that are just true enough to stop thought and end dissent. And anyway, the Nietzschean argument goes, it's not a glut of possibilities that kills motivation but rather a deep understanding of the true nature of things, the apprehension of truth and its terrors, which undoes the very condition that is required in order to act at all, tearing away the veil of illusion.) At the Globe, Bowden listens to Hamlet's soliloquy, to be or not, to suffer the slings or not, to take up arms or not, hearing those words the first time they were ever heard by anyone, and, with an acute feeling of crisis, he leaves the theater, ". . . the dread of something after death, the undiscover'd country, from whose bourn no traveler returns . . . ," having made his choice. He has chosen the sea of troubles, and, in doing so, he's also chosen the tragic condition, meaning he will suffer, and suffer knowingly, and decide to act anyway. Bowden went to the desert. He crossed the river, he crossed the line, he crossed the border. He chose dying colonies of bats and disappearing tortoises and vanishing populations of Sonoran pronghorn, he chose poor immigrants, he chose drugs and drug wars, chose torture and murder, chose rape in its violence and long aftermath, and he chose sex with children. That's the brute reality behind the veil of illusion in Bowden-land, and it's not unlike Susan Sontag's description of the tragic landscape, which "is about the emptiness and arbitrariness of the world, the ultimate meaninglessness of all moral values, and the terrifying rule of death and inhuman force." People underestimate how hard it is to say what you see . . . *the names go, the places too, just tiny details remain—the afternoon sunlight on a sidewalk on a cul-de-sac where a girl vanished or the short-haired gray cat a woman kept before she was raped and before she killed herself.* Throughout it all there's that rhythm, that earthy rhetoric, that eloquence in action. Perhaps Charles Bowden needed his music much like Prince Hamlet needs his play, to capture a conscience or two—his own first, I'm sure. What Jaspers says of Hamlet seems true of Bowden, that his work represents knowledge trembling at the edge of destruction. His shelf of books is his soliloquy.

Jericho tessellates in repeating patterns of narrative and image that aren't quite so Euclidean as the tiles you'd find on a floor in Marrakech. Ultimately the patterns emerge but the experience involves a certain kind of lostness and a tolerance for drift that's near and dear to the heart of good personal writing. Nothing's axiomatic, but that's okay. With Bowden wandering is wondering, a kind of inquiry, a "loose sally of the mind" of the sort described by Samuel Johnson, in defining the essay as "an irregular, undigested piece, not a regular, orderly performance." Interviews fail, good leads go nowhere, investigations lose momentum—a witness disappears, a lawyer dies—and promising stories simply don't pan out. All the roads in *Jericho* are rough. Even the title travels an enormous distance, from a tale of conquest and slaughter in the Old Testament to an anthem of civil rights in our century ... *in this version, one that wells up out of American bondage in the early nineteenth century, the story gets turned on its head. . . .* The spiritual is "Joshua Fit de Battle of Jericho." There's a haunting Paul Robeson recording, and Odetta's authority can't be denied, though I suspect if Bowden were alive he'd weigh in more knowledgeably and set me straight. *How do I explain this to myself?* To get to the anthem we first visit a garbage strike in Memphis; we hear the names of the two men who've been crushed and killed by the equipment that compacts the city's trash and now lie buried in pauper's graves, Echol Cole and Robert Walker; then we drift in time, turning back the clock to Martin Luther King's "Beyond Vietnam" speech, which takes a radical turn on the Jericho Road by flipping the parable of the good Samaritan;

and we must note not only that this speech is delivered on April 4, 1967, exactly a year to the day before King's murder, but also that the killing will be carried out by a fugitive who's crossed the border, coming up from Mexico, under the assumed name of Eric Galt. Anyway, that's how *Jericho* works. We follow the fragments, we pick up the pieces, we suffer under a load of doubt and uncertainty and yet muscle through on hints and clues and small hopes because that puzzling effort is the very weather of life. I'd no more silence this roughened voice than bring a statue in from the rain. A noble voice needs its weathers.

In *Jericho* Bowden's singular will to truth is tested by a new antagonist, the act of writing itself. *Once I was hungry for any glimpse inside this secret world. I would drive long distances; sit alone in a bleak motel room waiting for a call. I would spend money I did not have for a scrap of information. Sometimes a week would result in a single fact. I was ravenous. I am no longer hungry.* At one point we see Bowden noodling with a single sentence, a declarative sentence, the simplest kind there is, hoping it will somehow declare differently. "A man enters his house," Bowden writes, "and is shot dead." That's a sentence right out of a primer for children, children of an age when they still follow every word on the page with a loyal finger. Bowden turns the sentence over, and turns it again, but there's no way to write the story of a simple homecoming, this most ordinary and unremarkable thing, and also tell the truth. Imagine Bowden at his desk, 4 a.m., considering his options. He adds a bus, then two daughters, then a wife. *The real fear is not the killing.* The new sentence thickens with clauses, twisting like a wrestler trying to break a hold. Father, mother, two children, a house. You've drawn that picture. *It is that the killing might mean nothing at all.* Bowden tries again, adding a background detail, then the killers, two of them. Bowden works the sentence every which-way but none of the revisions conjure a different kind of day. Syntax won't save the man. At the end of the every sentence the man is dead.

I crossed the river about twenty years ago—I can't be exact about the date because I am still not sure what crossing really means except that you never come back.

The face of love would have no features if it weren't for the obstacles, and in Bowden's life and work, crossing the river, the line, the border seems to be where much of the scarring came from. Over the course of a long career he would return to these disputed spaces, borders and intersections that both join and separate, living in a kind of bardo that reads variously as a reality, a metaphysics, a history lesson, a geography, a lie, a frontier, a biblical narrative, a monster, an exile, a salvation, a myth, a truth. *I think maybe this is what history is, objects, words, scraps of things, a dash of whiskey and the claim of order and meaning.* His was a restless way of living, and yet *Jericho* drives home the fact that his life constellated around key themes of the sixties, a shape described in bold by race, sex, drugs, and a dubious war. The dark shadow of those essential American concerns, he discovered, was alive and well in his own backyard, in Tucson and El Paso, in Juárez and Nogales, and on down the line. There, too, he chose—he chose to engage, he chose to fight, he chose to serve a world in which truth was still very much at stake. Only someone who loves the world would bother, it seems to me, and maybe the emphasis here should fall on crossing itself. That's where he lived, not on one side or the other side, but in crossing, so walls of any kind, in Jericho or his own backyard or on the border we share with Mexico, were his natural enemy. If Montaigne claims to paint transience, perhaps we can say that Bowden paints crossing. If he were alive now would he have done another draft of *Jericho*? Changed anything? In that imaginary draft, a draft we'll never know, he might have fixed a problem and thus concealed it, or he might have answered his doubts rather than sharing them with us. It doesn't matter. The hand was stayed, and what's actually here is the art, the tragic vision, and the voice—mostly that: in fracture and rift *Jericho* finds a voice like no other, the voice of truth in all its troubled saying.

Jericho begins with the words: *I am dreaming*—and it ends this way:

There was a moment long ago when I drove deep into the north woods to pick up the papers of a retired congressman, the house nestled by a small lake in the cutover region where the Midwest had been gnawed to the ground and the sun was shining that day, the waters a jewel of blue, the house snug but not pretentious and I thought I will work my job, save and have this place in the woods and every day I will make the earth around me better, and every day the earth around me will feed me, and I will cease to really exist and become one with something else, melt into a thing of wonder.
    This did not happen.
    The walls came into my life . . .
    I have always been dreaming . . .
    In the dream, the walls do not tumble down.
    In the dream, they never were there at all.
    I am dreaming.

You see, the Jericho road
is a dangerous road.

MARTIN LUTHER KING JR.,
April 3, 1968

The hardest thing of all to see
is what is really there.

J. A. BAKER, *The Peregrine*

For we must consider that we shall be as a city upon a hill. The eyes of all people are upon us. So that if we shall deal falsely with our God in this work we have undertaken, and so cause Him to withdraw His present help from us, we shall be made a story and a by-word through the world. We shall open the mouths of enemies to speak evil of the ways of God, and all professors for God's sake. We shall shame the faces of many of God's worthy servants, and cause their prayers to be turned into curses upon us till we be consumed out of the good land whither we are going. And to shut this discourse with that exhortation of Moses, that faithful servant of the Lord, in his last farewell to Israel, Deut. 30. "Beloved, there is now set before us life and death good and evil," in that we are commanded this day to love the Lord our God, and to love one another, to walk in his ways and to keep his Commandments and his ordinance and his laws, and the articles of our Covenant with him, that we may live and be multiplied, and that the Lord our God may bless us in the land whither we go to possess it. But if our hearts shall turn away, so that we will not obey, but shall be seduced, and worship other Gods, our pleasure and profits, and serve them; it is propounded unto us this day, we shall surely perish out of the good land whither we pass over this vast sea to possess it.

JOHN WINTHROP, on board the *Arbella*, 1630

The reach fails against the blue sky, the gray sky and the black of night. Everything hangs there, the smell, the sound, the warmth of flesh, but beyond touch. The land hides in a haze and then down by the river vanishes into mist.

The reach, yes, the reach falls short.

Cold, gray, wet, rot, a slight breeze, gases seeping from plants dead beneath the water, the sucking sound of feet sloshing through muck.

A feather flutters down from the noise overhead.

White American pelicans ride on the waters of the marsh. Winter nears. Clouds of snow geese honk, various nations of ducks come and sandhill cranes begin to fall from the sky.

They come home to the place they lost and then found.

There is a history here of hunting.

The first men and women and children came after the ice retreated.

Later, pueblos of farmers and gatherers.

Then, Spaniards, then Mexicans with herds that devoured the land.

Then, Americans with real estate dreams and hearts of larceny.

By the time of the second big war, the place was a ruin, a biological desert of little use to anyone. The healing came, the fumbling, and now life oozes from the ground and clatters in the sky.

I come here to tear out the walls in my body.

I come here to die and live again as a beast or tree or bush.

This is my Jericho but I kill nothing but the part of me that has killed everything for so very long.

I am a fortress, yes, but I am tearing down my walls.

I see men hiding in blinds and watching over decoys.

They hold long guns.

They wear clothes that look like weeds and branches and dead leaves and when they rise up to fire it is as if they are coming out of the living earth bearing death.

The birds are flowing down, the men are ready, the dogs still, the waters cleansing.

I am on the river, I must follow this river, I must live the line.

They say the river is great.

They say the river is fierce.

They say the river is dying at our hand.

This is the iron law of Jericho where God tears down walls, deals death and yet everything continues.

And the horns play out and play down all the walls.

The hunters are part of the return of life here, they are the reason the place has returned from ruin and now they wait for the wings to bring life down from the sky.

So the birds have returned, as have their killers.

The walls, yes, the walls must come tumbling down.

But life and death stop for no one.

Men rise, the dogs are still, the guns fire.

Life flows down and washes my face.

The cold air warms my heart.

PART I

Peque Is on Ice

I am dreaming.

The black hawk calls, a man drives past in a Border Patrol truck as a woman in uniform leans out the passenger side door scanning the dirt for tracks.

Last night the owl did not hoot.

The ravens flew over before dawn and croaked down at my head.

Peque is still dead and on ice.

There is a man ahead of me in the checkout line.

The woman on his lower arm is all tears, blue tears dripping down his arm.

Another woman just above her has a large breast, spilling out over the man's brown skin.

Both women are blue; increasingly everything is blue.

And beautiful to my eye as I hold the neck of a bottle of red wine.

Everything makes sense, blue sense.

Except what I am told.

She is crying and she has a bare breast and she is blue ink.

Peque is on ice.

He was killed and his body left against the fence on the other side and no one seems to care except for those who knew him. Peque will never matter in all the talk of walls and lines and barriers, and that is why he stays in my head.

I noticed one wall and that wall led to other walls and they led to yet more walls. Soon I seem to live within walls.

The wall at Jericho falls on the advice of the Lord so that all the men and women and children in the city can be murdered. The wall at the Mexico border stands because the people of the United States fear Mexicans and want to keep them out. The walls between us as men and women as people and beasts as animals and plants as life and stone, these barriers exist because we worry that love may drown us and drag us unto a new ground where we will never be safe because our hearts will run free.

The walls tumble down. It is written in the book and the song says we must fulfill the book. But does that mean we blow the horns, and the walls fall and we kill everyone in the city? Or does it mean a blues horn floats over the walls, and they fall, and we become flesh of my flesh and blood of my blood and all the blood, plants, animals, things of the air, fish in the waters, rock and dirt underfoot, the very stones our brothers and sisters, the lion does sleep with the lamb, the guns go still, and all along the watchtowers the beacons get lit and sky goes to fire and our hearts warm?

We cross the line.

Ah, and soon, we will relax, lean back, we erase the line and face each other.

Delta

On October 9, 1964, President Lyndon Baines Johnson comes to New Orleans down by the river. He's a southern boy, a man who ran for years as a segregationist, a president who just that August had three young dead men come out of a dirt dam in Philadelphia, Mississippi, two white and one black, because they were trying to register black Americans to vote. Yes, Lyndon has a pedigree, and he goes into the banquet where there are two thousand well-heeled donors, all southern to their roots, and he starts talking down there by the levee. It's been hot lately because President Lyndon Baines Johnson has just rammed through the first significant civil rights bill since the Civil War and by this act he has forever altered the mathematics of southern elections because now it is obvious to everyone that the people whites used to lynch will vote in elections in the sweet by and by.

So he faces a crowd of rich white people who have pretty much run everything for centuries and he says that civil rights bill was passed by Congress.

And he says, "I am not going to let them build up hate and try to buy my people by appealing to their prejudice ...," and then he swings into a story about an old senator dying and on his death bed, this old pol—"whose name I won't call"— said he once begged the Speaker of the House to let him go home, to Mississippi, to make a single speech toward improving his ruined home state. The senator then went on to say, "Poor old Mississippi, they haven't heard a Democratic speech in thirty years. All they ever hear at election time is, 'Nigger! Nigger! Nigger!'"

They say the audience gasped. At first there was a scattered and kind of grudging applause and then the thing grew—the understanding—in the room that Johnson had said the obvious out loud, that all the stuff about southern rights, about restricting voting, about segregation, about separate but equal, was summed up and stood there naked when the president of the United States uttered three brutal words.

The local paper reported that Johnson said "Negro! Negro! Negro!" The *New York Times* did not report the moment. Later, when the people wrote books they said the president of the United States of America stood in front of two thousand rich folk in the city of New Orleans and said "Nigra! Nigra! Nigra!"

But he said nigger and the world shifted and a wall so old no one could remember when it first got thrown up, that wall came tumbling down.

Now I face another wall and no one seems willing to say what it is really about.

I no longer do lines of cocaine.

I no longer believe in the lines of borders.

I cease to care about the lines on my face.

On the ground, red ants swarm a dead scorpion by my foot.

The people once flowed north, a river of love and brimstone as padres walked into the dark kingdom of what they saw as Satan and spread Christianity behind Spanish pikes and swords. And crushed Indian nations with disease, labor and the lance. The Apache and Comanche raided south and ripped out the entrails of Spain's dominions and then of the new nation of Mexico. A US army conquered Mexico City and half the nation was forfeit. Pancho Villa raided one town in New Mexico and the US sent an entire army south into the dust.

Now the land is a wall and the river flows with fear and Christ is given lip service but the agents are given guns and the poor are prey and a threat to national security and there is a history here but politics erases the centuries of blood and theft and everything is talk ... of safety now and forever.

This is not a dream.

So, it will be written.

The Cranes

A crescent moon slides across the marsh as ducks float on the water. The cranes talk in the blackness. I did not expect the cranes but they flew into my life and now will not leave. They are migrants. They are without a country. They have a language that I struggle to learn. Slowly, hints of dawn come on. Mist dances across the water. And with the faint coming of the light the cranes soften their conversation.

Twenty minutes before sunrise, thousands of snow geese lift off the waters.

The cranes wait and bide their time.

Their voices carry across the waters.

They have come from Siberia.

They have come from Alaska.

They have come.

*   *   *

8 miles

I think I have mowed down sixty to eighty miles. The first day I am wobbly. The sun. The sounds. Insects around my face. A javelina bolts by the creek with its young trotting behind. The world is wrapped in gauze and I keep tearing at the film trying to reclaim a lost part of my life with scent and flavor and enormous fresh appetites.

That is the beginning. At first I wear old running shoes and then the constant stream crossings take their toll and I return to hiking boots and good wool socks. It is not quite a return to childhood, more the return of a clean season to my life.

Today, I see a gray hawk, three hepatic tanagers, hear a zone-tailed hawk, watch two vultures on the dead tree next to the rookery. But I fail to see a single great blue heron either at the rookery or flying along the creek.

The sky is overcast, a light shower drifts through in the morning. I fill the hummingbird feeders and they are swarming this morning. I have been gone nine days. At dusk I notice a great blue heron roosting on the power pole by the house. I struggle to only see and feel the concrete, a world of nouns as hard as pebbles that I can roll around in my hand for reassurance. I want my senses back and I think I can walk into them and past every barrier I have created with my life. I do not answer the phone and I ignore messages. I try not to go to town or speak. I lock my binoculars at a random spot on a distant tree and simply see the leaves but look for nothing, nothing at all, just a green shimmer flooding my mind.

I want to belong. I just cannot say what I want to belong to. I am certain about what I am leaving.

Borders.

Walls.

And thought.

This last one is beyond my words. I write about leaving thought but cannot yet capture with words the sensation of leaving thought behind me like roadkill. If I keep moving, I know I can do it. The sparrows moving through the dried stalks of Johnson grass pull me out of my skin and into the thicket where the ladder-backed woodpecker pounds a dead limb on a tree and a goldfinch watches from on high at the top of a cottonwood and then slowly the names of the birds fall off them like scales and I look at them and am with them.

This will take time. But I feel it coming.
During the day the space is blue.
At night black.
And always warm to the touch.

The Jericho Road

The facts do not matter. A man is gone, David Hartley, his wife says the man is dead. David Hartley becomes a matter of legend, and this legend erases David Hartley and erases me.

There are reports of violence spilling across the border. Politicians insist that the border must be secured because American lives are at risk.

I see things differently.

The dead are Mexicans.

The frightened are Americans.

The violence is a tidal wave sweeping all before it and it rolls south and murders Mexico.

Monsters are called for but the land refuses to provide them.

They must be invented, and American history is a series of self-created monsters. Perhaps the nation's greatest folk art. There was in the beginning the wilderness where Satan lurked and where the city on the hill could be toppled by demons spewing from the forests. There were the dreaded savages, also lost to Satan, who must die so that God and the godly might live. There were bestial blacks who might rise up in rebellion against their enslavement and people who thought it was obvious God intended them to work in the fields to be under the dominion of white men. There was of course Demon Rum, and even worse after the Civil War came socialists and anarchists and the Yellow Peril and then unions and then Communists and then Terrorists and their offspring "Illegal Immigrants."

The land groans under the weight of its monsters.

There is the fear in childhood of the night.

The dream of drowning; the nightmare of execution.

Monsters that come from within us and shove our personal wars into the face of the world. And the terror comes not from the question of violence spilling across the border. It comes from that word, border.

Borders must be gone. I will have none of them. The line between me and the fly buzzing round my head, this line must cease.

This is when I begin walking the Jericho road.

Cranes

On a winter morning, I get up by the river and step outside and the irrigated field next to the bosque of cottonwoods is full of sandhill cranes. Years before, I had seen a petroglyph of a crane dancing, a snatch of life recorded before Columbus cleared port.

They move in a stately manner.

They are very large.

And there is always the chance of a dance.

I remember reading in an ornithological journal the account of a couple that worked at a refuge for sandhills in Wisconsin. The female cranes would crowd around the husband and shunt the wife aside.

Their call is in the sky, a ghost of some forgotten past.

The two cranes of North America, sandhill and whooping, almost left the skies empty because of the killing. In the case of the whooping crane they are still almost ghosts. Illinois saw its last one in 1891, they vanished from Iowa by 1911, Minnesota in 1917. After the killing, ornithologists figured that between 1870 and 1900, 90 percent of the whooping cranes on earth were destroyed. By 1912, maybe a hundred still lived and thirty-six of these survivors were shot in the next six years.

I roll these numbers around in my head when I hear talk

of violence spilling across borders and of the need to secure borders and of the danger posed by aliens on the land.

There is a spring in this borderland.

The spring is on no map and waits in the desert, the spring seeps blood among the lilies of the valley and bones surround the red pond where the earth hemorrhages all the wounded dreams and overhead at night the cries of cranes shake the darkness.

After midnight, under a moonless sky a birdsong shakes the skin of the planet.

I fly with ten billion migratory birds hailing from a thousand species and half of us will die each journey and none of us will build the wall. We have no papers, ever.

Delta

I remember in my childhood connecting things and being told such things cannot be connected. A turtle in the mud by the creek meant more than God. New Orleans could not survive because there was too much water and not enough dirt. My aunt is buying crabs in the French Quarter market, the levee is right there and on the river ships ride above my head.

Now New Orleans and border are joined in my head and nothing will convince me otherwise. New Orleans began as a barrier. The site was seized to cork the river from foreign invaders—anyone not French. Then it was stocked with whores and convicts and when they failed to produce enough to feed themselves, Germans were brought in and settled just above the outpost. The ground was French, then Spanish, then French again and then American. Before that it was a splatter of native peoples and nearby black villages rose up, the creations of escaped slaves. But New Orleans, sitting barely above sea level, had to have walls, huge walls and they were called levees and they multiplied and went on and on until finally, by the mid-twentieth century, the Lower Mississippi loses its ability to protect New Orleans from the fist of storms.

And along the river and in sloughs, whooping cranes, and along the river and in the old growth forest, ivory-billed woodpeckers, and both vanish from the watershed as the levees go up and up, the cranes barely surviving in one colony on the Texas coast and the woodpeckers probably departing into eternity.

The levees stand to make a city safe as the city sinks and seas rise and the delta that guarded the city is destroyed acre by acre and day by day.

None of this connects with the border or the wall or the death of the delta or the death of the ancient town.

I remember in my childhood connecting things and being told such things cannot be connected.

I hear Jericho and the walls tumbling, the trumpets, the others, the killings, yes, the killings.

I have no clear idea. That is the improvement. I have put my trumpet down and have lost the desire to enter Jericho and kill every man, woman and child.

El Sicario

The man in the veil leans forward. He holds a pen. On his lap is a sketchbook with a fine black moleskin cover. His thick fingers begin to draw in sepia ink. He says nothing. The veil walls him off. He is alone in this moment, just the pen, the paper, and the images in his head.

Soft light filters through the window. The river dribbles a half mile away and then Juárez.

He makes a faint rubbing sound on the paper.

He is looking down at an intersection, the two-lane streets neatly delineated with painted stripes to segregate traffic.

He turns the page, the pen moves fast, now there is a house and garage and a car being cut off.

Next, he has a flurry of vehicles all moving into place to block and isolate one particular car.

Off to the side, someone is watching it all like a movie director.

In the stillness of the room as the pen slides on the paper, there is silence punctured by a burst of gunfire on the page as the isolated car becomes a scene of death.

He is finished with this sketch: a perfect hit.

His veil gently sways as he examines his creation.

This is all part of a movie.

It will get me to Venice.

But not beyond the reach of Jericho.

I drive two thousand miles. I hunt the great fear.

I carry my binoculars, bird books, a tree guide, and a bed-roll.

I dream of sleeping out under the stars.

My camping stove can boil water in two minutes or less and coffee must be made before dawn, before even the gray light.

Rules cannot be broken.

I am walking down a street near the bridge approach to El Paso. A Tarahumara woman and her small daughters sit on the sidewalk. They glow like flowers in long dresses shouting colors. They are eating garbage filched from the sidewalk, their hands a mash of rejected tacos which they shove in their mouths. Their skin is dark and dirty, their hair lank.

I hardly bat an eye. The other beggars have become invisible also.

Killings start to slip past me.

Often, there is a mother or brother or sister nearby. The women weep and their faces look like broken windows. Flies buzz over the fresh blood.

On a dirt hillside in a slum, I am distracted from the kill site by the bleating of goats rummaging through the trash heap of a gully.

I do not approve of this slippage.

Jericho

The lines solve nothing. There are so many of us and every day there are more people that have no function in the world, people without work or pleasure or purpose. The people with money do not see them, the people with no purpose exist as crimes.

This has happened before.

And Abram was very rich in cattle, in silver, and in gold. And he went on his journeys from the south even to Bethel, unto the place where his tent had been at the beginning, between Bethel and Hai; (Gen. 13.2–3)

And in Genesis the men and beasts overwhelmed the land.

And Lot also, which went with Abram, had flocks, and herds, and tents. And the land was not able to bear them, that they might dwell together: for their substance was great, so that they could not dwell together. And there was a strife between the herdmen of Abram's cattle and the herdmen of Lot's cattle.... (Gen. 13.5–7)

A solution is found: sharing. This is before the walls, before Jericho comes tumbling down. This is in the beginning.

And Abram said unto Lot, Let there be no strife, I pray thee, between me and thee, and between my herdmen and thy herdmen; for we be brethren. Is not the whole land before thee? separate thyself, I pray thee, from me: if thou wilt take the left hand, then I will go to the right; or if thou depart to the right hand, then I will go to the left. . . . (Gen. 13.8–9)

In 1964, when Lyndon Johnson is in the midst of his civil rights bill battle, he hosts clergy at the White House to marshal some moral force behind the idea that all Americans have equal rights. He tells the preachers they must "reawaken the conscience of your beloved land." And he reaches into Genesis for the tale of Abraham and Lot.

Abraham and Lot, uncle and nephew, kept the peace by separating before their herdsmen came to blows. But there are bad stories about Lot in some books.

El Pastor

Asylum will no longer be offered.

He tears into three steaks, one piled atop the other, and explains that the money is vanishing and he can no longer feed the people he keeps in the crazy place. There are about one hundred and twenty of them—brains gone from drugs, brains gone from beatings, brains gone from glue, brains gone from paint sniffing—and now he is running out of food. He still travels to churches, he continues, and preaches and passes the plate. But the church members are vanishing as their jobs disappear and the plate comes back with very little cash because no one has any money.

Last week, when he exiled twenty people from his asylum, he picked the ones he thought had the best chance of surviving on the street where they could beg and, come night, sleep in cardboard boxes. Two refused to go. They said they'd rather be hungry in the asylum than be out there.

Monday, he explains, he was going to shut it all down, give up after years of work. But his wife would not let him.

She said, "You are my hero."

And he believed her.

When he prayed, God, also, would not let him.

He tears into his pile of steaks.

He is prone to getting messages from God.

And he likes to eat.

But still, the asylum is ending. Safe places are getting hard to come by.

So he prays.

And eats with gusto.

His name is Jose Antonio Galvan.

He is called El Pastor.

He tells me I have ten years before Satan takes me.

Jericho

In Jericho, the priests circled the wall for six days with the Ark of the Covenant. They had just come over Jordan—the Lord had split the river, just as He had divided the Red Sea forty years before. God led them, though he needed the help of the whore Rahab. Moses could not enter the Promised Land and Joshua took over and led the people of Israel, and the Jordan River split, and they crossed and came to the walled city of Jericho over three thousand years ago and they brought death.

The city itself, the actual spot on earth, has been home to people for eleven thousand years and is the lowest city on earth. God, after its ruin, forbade it ever being rebuilt. But it was rebuilt on a nearby site.

And the walls came tumbling down.

Now Jericho was straitly shut up because of the children of Israel: none went out, and none came in. (Josh. 6:1)

The wall made the world safe until the walls came tumbling down.

And the LORD said unto Joshua, See, I have given into thine hand Jericho, and the king thereof, and the mighty men of valour. And ye shall compass the city, all ye men of war, and go round about the city once. Thus shalt thou do six days. And seven priests shall bear before the ark seven trumpets of rams' horns: and the seventh day ye shall compass the city seven times, and the priests shall blow with the trumpets. (Josh. 6:2–4)

It is never explained what the point of seven priests is, or of the ram's horns, or why the King of Jericho must die along with his men of valor and almost every other living thing in the city.

Drones now fly the Mexican border, each with its bulbous head, blue band, various radar snouts searching with US Customs and Border Protection spelled out on the white fuselage. One comes over the hill and rustles the leaves on the live oaks, the craft moving almost silently, skimming as it hunts for the enemies of the state, a machine working for freedom by catching people trying to escape doom.

The air feels fresh from the rain, the drone almost purrs as it rolls over the hill and plunges down into the meat of the hunt.

And it shall come to pass, that when they make a long blast with the ram's horn, and when ye hear the sound of the trumpet, all the people shall shout with a great shout; and the wall of the city shall fall down flat, and the people shall ascend up every man straight before him. (Josh. 6:5)

Railroad Man

The fears come and kill the freedoms. The Alien and Sedition Acts of 1798, the fugitive slave laws, the suspension of habeas corpus by President Lincoln during the Civil War, the Espionage Act of World War I that landed Eugene Debs, sixty-four years old, a ten-year sentence for telling his fellow citizens to resist the draft and being called "a traitor to his country" by President Woodrow Wilson.

Debs had stood before a crowd in Canton, Ohio, and said, "It is extremely dangerous to exercise the constitutional right of free speech in a country fighting to make democracy safe in the world."

He is tried for that speech and he tells the court, "Your Honor, years ago I recognized my kinship with all living beings, and I made up my mind that I was not one bit better than the meanest on earth. I said then, and I say now, that while there is a lower class, I am in it, and while there is a criminal element I am of it, and while there is a soul in prison, I am not free."

Debs is largely forgotten. Woodrow Wilson often recalled him as a liberal soul.

Wilson himself had struggled to keep the United States out of the big war. He feared the conflict would weaken the white nations and unleash the lesser breeds. As he explained to

Frank Lansing, his secretary of state, "White civilization's domination over the world rested largely on our ability to keep this country intact."

When they tried Eugene Debs in 1918 and called him a traitor, he represented himself in court. He called not a single witness. He asked to speak and he spoke for two hours.

Debs said:

> Your honor, I have stated in this court that I am opposed to the form of our present government; that I am opposed to the social system in which we live; that I believe in the change of both but by perfectly peaceable and orderly means. . . .
>
> I am thinking this morning of the men in the mills and factories; I am thinking of the women who, for a paltry wage, are compelled to work out their lives; of the little children who, in this system, are robbed of their childhood, and in their early, tender years, are seized in the remorseless grasp of Mammon, and forced into the industrial dungeons, there to feed the machines while they themselves are being starved body and soul. . . .
>
> Your honor, I ask no mercy, I plead for no immunity. I realize that finally the right must prevail. I never more fully comprehended than now the great struggle between the powers of greed on the one hand and upon the other the rising hosts of freedom. I can see the dawn of a better day of humanity. The people are awakening. In due course of time they will come into their own.
>
> When the mariner, sailing over tropic seas, looks for relief from his weary watch, he turns his eyes toward the Southern Cross, burning luridly above the tempest-vexed ocean. As the midnight approaches the Southern Cross begins to bend, and the whirling worlds change their places, and with starry finger-points the Almighty marks the passage of Time upon the dial of the universe; and though no

bell may beat the glad tidings, the look-out knows that the midnight is passing—that relief and rest are close at hand.

Let the people take heart and hope everywhere, for the cross is bending, midnight is passing, and joy cometh with the morning.

They took his vote away for life—he got over a million ballots when he ran for president in 1912. He did his federal stretch in Atlanta—in 1920 he got almost a million write-in votes for president. His sentence was commuted in 1921 after Wilson left office.

He was a railroad man out of Indiana.

He is not remembered much.

The Cranes

There was a belief in the ancient world that some or all of the shapes of letters in the Greek alphabet came from a careful observation of cranes. For example, the letters lambda, alpha and upsilon were thought to be inspired by various crane body positions. There are stones in Sweden incised five thousand years ago with dancing cranes. I walk along the river, the sandhill cranes have arrived and I carry in my hand a booklet, *Sandhill Crane Display Dictionary: What Cranes Say with Their Body Language*.

The dictionary warns that it is based on a single dialect and may not be accurate for other groups.

Juárez

The pink salmon rests near the sliced red onion. The fall weather brings sunny days and crisp nights. There is no breeze today, and the still air hangs over the valley lined with fields and groves.

The lawyer laughs and says, "This guy comes in, and he's got a problem. He got behind on his protection payments in Juárez and so they started burning his restaurants. He can't pay anymore because business is way off. So they take his six-year-old daughter. Then he gets a call and the kid's on the line and she says, 'Daddy, they're hurting my parts,' and then this guy comes on the line and he says, 'We don't want money. We want you to come in and we'll give up your daughter and then we will kill you. That way everyone else will know they must pay.'"

The lawyer pauses and sips some red wine. There's a white also cooling in an ice bucket and there are bagels and scones and fresh butter and fruit. It is a perfect day and the patio feels clean and crisp.

Earlier, he'd explained how security in Ascension, a small town in northern Chihuahua, had changed after the kidnapping and lynching. Now there is a number and if it is called it rings every phone in town and then everyone goes out on the street and all ways in and out of Ascension are slammed closed and so no bad guy can get away with bad things now.

That's the idea anyway.

But now he's back to the guy and his six-year-old daughter.

"The guy," he continues, "figures if he turns himself in as an exchange for his daughter, they will kill them both. But that's not the real problem he faced. He's got three other kids and so if he gives himself up and is killed, who is going to take care of them?"

No one asks what decision the guy finally made.

The red wine is dry, the chilled white has a slight burr to it.

The salmon, pink and cool, tastes good in the air of early fall.

Falcon Lake

On September 30, 2010, David and Tiffany Hartley travel with jet skis from McAllen, Texas, to Falcon Lake, which straddles the border between Texas and Mexico. He's thirty, she's twenty-nine and they have been married eight years. There are no children. She stays at home, he works in the oil industry. They get a ticket in Rio Grande City for an expired tag on their trailer. They stop at Subway in Roma for a bite and Tiffany notes two Border Patrol agents are also eating. Later she says, "Me being a Christian and believing in God, I believe he lined all that up, he lined up the traffic stop, he lined up us going to Subway and having the Border Patrol there so my story would be supported by events that happened."

They launch at the public ramp in Zapata on a quiet Thursday afternoon.

A short time later, Tiffany comes back. She runs up to a man mowing his lawn, and he places a call to 911.

The operator asks, "Are you sure your husband got shot?"

"Yes. In the head."

Though he is wearing a life vest, his body is not recovered. Though his Sea-Doo is virtually unsinkable, it also is not recovered.

Tiffany Hartley cannot describe the attackers except that

they were pirates in three boats. She never wavers on this point. One boat with armed men pauses in the water less than ten feet from her and her murdered husband.

She appears on numerous television shows.

She says she is not seeking justice.

She says she simply wants her husband's body back.

Her voice is even.

Her face looks almost blank.

When asked if she had anything to do with her husband's death, she does not take offense but answers calmly that she did not.

12.2 miles

I leave at six a.m. with a fifteen-pound pack and walk 12.2 miles, five of them through the hills north of the creek. The numbers matter to me, proof of some kind of change. Or at least of some effort at change. The last three miles on Blue Haven Road just about finish me off because of the heat and my failure to drink much water. I try to sit down but simply collapse under a mesquite. When I finally pour a liter on my head, I slowly revive. It is over a hundred degrees. I wonder if I can make it back and decide I must make it back because I would rather fall over dead than stop and ask for help. I do not think this through. My decision is made instantly.

In the hills I see two gray hawks hunting through the mesquite. When I return to the road by the creek I can hear a black hawk keening.

I wonder about several things. On the three-mile walk back after my collapse, I simply wonder if I will make it. I also wonder why I do not care. My mind floats, I cannot seem to lock onto a thought and my vision becomes fuzzy. The light storms my brain. I wear no hat. I am reeling as I walk.

As I grow weaker, I think I grow stronger. This is a crusade I have launched against myself.

Each day I hit the earth harder. I walk with more weight and more hills and each day I feel like I am breaking apart. I seek this sensation. I am smelting down my body and will hammer out a new being on an anvil.

The days tumble one into another and now all I am is walking. Everything else, including writing this note, is a minor matter. Like memory and thought, it has ceased to interest me.

I can hardly abide people. I no longer go to town if possible and I shop at lonely hours when the stores are empty.

I meet a friend in the local tavern and sit at the bar. I can hardly tolerate the place and the happy faces over drinks. I feel as if I am drowning. When I return to the creek, night has fallen and I sit outside as bats careen by my head and moonrise is a faint sliver.

I feel birds now rather than see them.

I sit outside and stare, a book open on my lap but unread, and from time to time l look up and always there are ducks or a heron or hawks, always some form gliding past me. I am beginning to sense things. I do not study things. I join things.

One moonless night, I leave the house and walk. I cannot see my hand in front of my face. I stop for five minutes to let my eyes adjust and then shuffle on with the barest sense of rock and tree. I have a headlamp but do not turn it on. I sense this is forbidden.

A cuckoo screeches in the blackness and it feels like the embrace of something that has been missing from my life for years.

Oscar

He weighs over four hundred pounds but I do not write that. He is hiding from the Aztecas who wish to kill him but that also I do not write. He is subject to violent episodes and this I lightly touch on. And he has killed but I do not ask the number of his dead.

His hair is cropped short and his head looks like a bowling ball, the body massive with folds of fat. The voice a monotone, quiet and precise. The eyes are brown and cold. He is a man who sees everything and yet belongs to nothing.

I first met him as he raced toward me across a creosote desert on an ATV. And then we ate lunch, $60 of fried pork. He wears a dark blue T-shirt that says COME TO BIG DADDY. The copper vats full of hot grease have turned green with age, the Mexicans tending to the frying meat use big paddles and the air hangs heavy with lard. The road is lined with junkyards and truck terminals. The tables inside with men with grease under their nails and company prostitutes and bottles of beer.

A red table blazes in my eyes and the white walls have yellow paint outlining each tier of blocks. The room has the feel of a cafeteria—big, noisy and everyone eating pork out of the vats. He looms over me in his chair. I'm six foot four but I look like a tyke next to him as I make notes. He crosses his arms and stares straight ahead as he speaks.

He was part of the inner circle, the council of a half dozen that ruled the gang, took orders from the police and by extension from the drug cartel. They did killings when requested. They smuggled dope north, guns south. They worked with the Border Patrol and soldiers out of Fort Bliss. This is all matter-of-fact to him.

Now the Mexican army is in town killing people, he says softly.

And he is hiding.

It takes two chickens, two dozen eggs and a gallon or two of milk to keep him fit. He is calm now, released from the rebar cage he spent months in. The drugs have drained from his body.

He can now remember. For years there was the gang, then he crossed over, married, had a kid, got a job as a trucker. But the schedule was hard and soon speed took over and this confused his thoughts and brought anger. He beat the wife, got thrown in jail, attacked the judge in the court. And then was tossed back across the line. And was defenseless. His family would have none of him since he had attacked them. Leaving the gang meant a contract on his life. And so he would end up in the desert in the cage with other crazy people. That's how I met him. He'd be detoxed, slowly promoted and then helped out. Had a little room outside the wall with his own bed and a small television. Plus, a girlfriend.

He tends to small things, like putting out the blankets on the creosote bushes around the crazy place so they can dry and then, when the moment is right, he takes the ATV with a small trailer behind and roars out in the desert. The crazy people stream over the wall, gather and pile the blankets on his rig. He rides with a straw hat and dark sunglasses.

And he thinks about God, and the Mexican army, and killing people, and his hunger for drugs, and how the drugs make him want to hit and kill people.

The voice so soft as he sits and devours *carnitas* and almost whispers of his life. He has killed, led a gang, been jailed, deported, drugged and now he is in the crazy place and not yet thirty.

I give El Pastor a hundred dollars to feed the crazy people with. He hears of it, demands his share. His old anger reappears.

He crosses over, is arrested, jailed again.

Then tossed back.

No one wants him.

And he cannot hide on the street. Or even feed himself.

So he returns, to go back into the cage for months until the anger ebbs.

He decides to become a minister. Each Saturday a seminarian comes out to the crazy place to teach him the word of God. He is determined to find the path.

He moves quietly through the yard with the crazy people. He towers over them and they seem to regard him as a peaceful whale. His face blank, eyes almost hooded, that voice soft as he moves around the people who talk to themselves, the legless ones who are spread out on the ground like blankets, the hyperactive woman in the security guard uniform who always smiles and tugs at the sleeve of each person she encounters, the gang girl from Los Angeles who speaks clearly and puzzles over the fragments her young life has become.

El Pastor tells me he is dangerous.

And then he has him drive as we leave the crazy place. The car sags deeply on the driver's side.

His name is Oscar.

I never see him smile.

Oscar lives with dust in the air. There is the smell of shit and urine and dirty clothing and a faint coating in the air of grease from the asylum kitchen. When I first meet him there is no electrical connection, no heating, no cooling and water comes by truck. His little television lives off a car battery. Most of the walled compound is bare dirt with dreams of gardens dancing in El Pastor's head. At night, there are a few kerosene lamps and muffled cries. The day brings dust and wind and heat and cold and always flies.

There is a photograph of the moment we met. He is on the ATV. In the background on the mountain is a copy of the Uffington horse, a giant white steed. I am standing surrounded by crazy people gathering blankets. His eyes hide behind sunglasses and his face is blank.

He is the movie that is never made with a story that has no moral.

The Foolish Life

There came a moment in my late twenties—maybe, the third time I spun a car off a curve and went flying through the air, or maybe it was some other moment—when I suddenly thought I had an idea. The idea was this: I should not have a foolish death. I began to drive more sensibly after that and to the best of my ability, limited to be sure, I reined in my vices and tried to flog them with work, endless bouts of work.

I think I had it all wrong.

The thing to avoid is not a foolish death.

It is a foolish life.

A life of caution, a life of opportunities ignored, money banked, a life of seat belts, regular checkups, no collisions, and not enough hangovers.

They are not the problem in life, they are the consequence of life.

Now I feel better about my careless ways.

This morning a diamondback hardly moves by my foot as it slowly warms in the dirt of the road. I stand there and watch as it flicks its tongue, taking my measure. By the creek a javelina explodes from a mass of morning glories, a gray hulk leaping through the blue flowers. The Johnson grass hides the deer from prying eyes.

Hawk

Down the river, a red-tailed hawk finishes off a rabbit in the morning light. The heat begins to come on, the sands of the river blaze a white light. The hawk sits on the sand and crunches a blood-flecked bone with its beak. The Rio Grande runs low now, barely a channel snaking across the empty bottom. The dams have shut off the flow. A few mallards paddle, the sandpipers have moved on. Finally, the red tail flaps off the sands and lands on a low nearby tree. I approach. It does not stir. I can sense a sickness in the bird.

I sit down and wait.

I remember one evening coming off a murder, one that seems to have kept me up for days interviewing and failing. I can't even remember the house or the corpse or the name. You think this will never happen, that these moments will never fade, but the dead begin to pile up on each other and then you have a heap of corpses and then the whole mound of flesh blurs and the names go, the places too, just tiny details remain—the afternoon sunlight on a sidewalk on a cul-de-sac where a girl vanished or the short-haired gray cat a woman kept before she was raped and before she killed herself.

That evening I went to a party. It was early in the fall, the nights were still warm. The party was out back and everyone was sitting on benches and smoking and drinking. There were candles burning for light and off in the corners one or two joints were consumed. The women were dressed casually but they had changed their clothes since work. I sat down with a group of people and suddenly I had nothing to say. I could not join their conversation and I could not listen to their conversation. I was at some other place with my dead.

A woman I knew asked, "What's wrong with you?"

I said I was tired. I said, I guess I'm poor company.

I didn't say what I thought, that I would like to kill everyone at this party.

I made excuses and left.

I never really came back.

That is when I finally went south though it was years before I understood this simple fact.

As I get up the hawk flaps away. It only goes a short distance and lands in the water and just sits there. There is no breeze and in the dead calm there are no thermals for the hawk to ride. But I sense it is more than that.

The hawk is sick and must back away from things and heal.

Or the hawk will die.

It stares at me with its black eye.

Falcon Lake

His tattoos are fading, the gray hair close-cropped, his beard grizzled. He does not smile. The window air conditioner groans as the aged compressor struggles against the heat. He rents cheap rooms where men come to fish, drink and sleep and escape the rules of their women. The walls speak of stale air and of freedom. In the corner is a clutter of old fans, the check-in counter a jumble.

He says, "You have to know the rules and then there is no problem."

He has the look of a man who hates rules and authority because he spent his working life obeying rules and his superiors.

He says, "You know when to leave, when the Mexican fishermen go."

He says, "I've fished the lake for years and never had a problem."

He scoffs at Mrs. Hartley's story. He goes on the lake and upriver to San Ygnacio on a pontoon boat and has no problem. Her jet ski can go 75 mph.

The woman comes in. She has tired skin, dyed red hair, thin lips and she gets behind the counter with him and almost snorts contempt at the mention of the Hartleys.

The lake is a sea of peace if you know the rules and part of the rules tell you the best fishing is in Mexico and if other people on the lake have not come for the fishing that is no-body's business.

People come here to escape the center. To escape the wives. The rules. The hours. They come here to the edge and speak of the heart of the country. All along the line refugees gather from the center of the United States and insist they are the real United States but that the real United States is outlawed and so they must come to the edge and fish. And own guns.

In the fifties, when Falcon Lake came into being as a joint US/ Mexico venture to control flooding in the lower Rio Grande Valley, it prompted a new migration into the United States of America. Great Kiskadee, *Pitangus sulphuratus*, a tyrant flycatcher, began colonizing upriver all the way to Del Rio, the spot where the Texas brush country ends and the dry limestone plateau takes over. South Texas is the Great Kiska-dee's northern frontier and it extends into South America. They will dive into water for prey and then beat it to death against a branch. They chase other birds, including hawks, from their territory.

Nobody made much fuss over that invasion.

Nobody made much fuss over the braceros program to bring in the crops when Americans were off killing in World War II and the farms became shorthanded.

Now there is a fuss.

* * *

7.3 miles

At noon hot air sags with humidity, the sky gray and still. A black hawk flies overhead, another keens again on the same dead limb by the creek. The crossing is a ruin of mud and blocked by a cottonwood log from high water last night. Along the creek a huge limb—ten or fifteen feet around—

has fallen off a cottonwood. The green leaves are limp. The creek bed is scoured and smears of fresh mud coat the banks. A heron flaps off and moves downstream at my approach.

I see no one and find few footprints save deer.

The storm announces the beginning of the monsoon. I heard the creek rise in the night and walked down naked to the rushing brown water that played in the glare of the flashlight. Now the beached cottonwood limb blocking the road testifies to the vanished flow. The fence is also gone and the horses wander the road eating out of the ditches. The chiggers will soon be in the thickets and meadows.

The watercress is ripped from the stream and will not reemerge until fall.

The heat breaks, the air mellows and scent replaces dust. I think I can hear the leafless oaks on the hillside beginning to revive, the sluggish movement of sap finally seeping into the branches. I begin to see black-bellied whistling ducks for the first time, their long pink legs glowing in the stream.

I find broken branches along the creek and two miles upstream a large cottonwood knocked down across the trail in a dead man's sprawl. The water runs muddy.

I sit down and stare as the sun skips along the riffles and my mind empties. A doe and her fawn move slowly off into the sea of Johnson grass, the shadow of a vulture falls across my life.

There is no reason.

Memories crowd the new scents in the air that followed the rain, trailing a perfume of life. I am walking through a small grove in Illinois. I think I am seven. A brook lightly moves through the thickets and I follow it, the water sloshing into my black and white gym shoes. Brown leaves from the oaks carpet the ground and when I step out of the water they crunch under my feet. It is fall, the sky overcast, and the land flat. The trees are huge, centuries of oaks towering over me.

I look for tracks, for some sign of beasts. I dream of deer but settle for a cottontail that bolts out of a thicket.

The woods end, the brook flows into a culvert that vanishes underneath a new subdivision.

I turn back.

Now I understand.

I made the right decision then, but years of errors followed. I must make amends with myself.

The rows of new houses stand like a stockade.

My walking keeps growing and ebbing.

There was a time when I worked in Chicago and would walk for hours like a beast pacing its cage in a zoo. In the west I tried to salvage my sanity by journeys of a hundred or two hundred miles on foot. One day, by a desert water hole, I decided I was going everywhere and getting nowhere. I began walking mile after mile and then sitting down until the food ran out and the anger left me.

I buy a sleeping bag, pad, stove and coffee cup. I pack a knife and fork. I carry these things always, along with a gallon of water, bird books and a tree guide, and a rainproof jacket. It is essential that I can stay out there forever.

This last is not to be discussed.

The Cranes

The sandhill cranes nest in Siberia, Alaska and Canada and then go all the way to Cuba and Mexico to winter. Most of them pause at a seventy-five-mile stretch of the Platte River in Nebraska and organize for the rest of the journey. They live decades. With luck, they may get one chick to adulthood each year. In China, statues of cranes flanked the emperor's throne. In Japan, they are seen as links to the eternal heavens, symbols of fidelity and prosperity.

Five million years ago, their ancestors were larger, ate meat and loved to kill the early version of the horse. All memory of this is gone and now they are links to the gods. And to dance.

The people of the Australian outback notice the dance, the people in China and Asia see it also, people in ancient Greece and Rome are brought up short, men and women on the Hopi mesas and in the pueblos of the Rio Grande see the dance.

The gods watch the dance, the emperors watch the dance. One of the first acts of a sandhill crane is to teach the young to dance so that the beat of life flows endlessly into the world.

I stand by a marsh along the river. The cranes are making calls to each other. There is no one here. In Japan, it was thought that a sage could visit the gods on a crane's back. But if he could become a crane, he could pass through that point in the sky and join eternity.

Juárez

His boy lives in a cage but there is nothing to be done about that at the moment. So he has a Seagram's 7 in the glow of a Tiffany-colored glass dome in the old bar near the river where Pancho Villa was said to drink and never did. The boy went to Juárez with a friend to have his truck repaired and just when he was about to cross the bridge on his return the Mexican army arrested him and charged him with carrying kilos of marijuana on his lap. Two Mexican boys saw the army plant the drugs in the truck. One boy disappeared, the other boy and his father were murdered. None of this matters now that the two men are in the cage. They have both been tortured, they have both confessed, they have been sentenced to five years.

The father crosses four or five days a week and visits. He pays the guards, warden, everyone, he pays the cartel member that rules the cellblock. He can protect his son. He hears many stories. Everyone has been tortured, everyone has been framed, and none of this matters.

Today, he took along his son's twenty-year-old wife and she says, "All these men who torture have mothers. What would their mothers think?"

The father is not bitter. He is learning Mexico. Each day he crosses the bridge and there is a young girl there begging and he gives her money. They have become friends of a sort.

He says, "She's not in school. In time, she'll either become a drug addict or a prostitute. I have daughters the same age and she made me a purse to give them."

Then he sips his drink and sighs.

That night I sit outside and sip wine while a blazing moon rides over the border. I write the father about the moon and he replies he is watching it through his telescope.

The peace of earth hangs over the line as three vehicles glide to a stop in a working-class neighborhood in Juárez. They leave fifteen dead at a party. The federal police come by three minutes later but ignore the wounded trying to flag them down. The ambulances are very late in arriving and a nine-year-old girl dies from her wounds.

The ground is white with the moon.

*   *   *

El Pastor points to the cemetery where he has a plot, his hole he says, and then explodes with "I love it," his way of punctuating anything hard in life. He is turning sixty-one today and he is full of the common notions about life—that it goes by fast, that just about when you understand life, well, you die and meet Jesus, but somehow that all seems a stretch. At his house they are setting up for the party and when he left to fetch another guest, the speakers were booming "Sixteen Candles" and El Pastor thought, my God, I was seventeen when I met my wife and that is the first song she played for me and suddenly he could feel the endless line of years that became his life.

The party is outside by the Greek columns and archway— the grand entrance to the garden. The house backs right up to the south bank of the Rio Grande and dirt bikes roar on the levee while egrets feed in the slack water of the river. An old man in shorts and a T-shirt walks back and forth on the levee with a huge staff in his hand. Eight mallards flap past overhead.

The air sags with smoke off two grills as the chicken and steaks cook. Tina Turner belts out "Proud Mary," and the song—"but I never saw the good side of the city"—floats over the thirty or forty people gathered for the event. Two fountains gurgle from the wall separating the house lots. Christ stares down from the mountain that punctures the borders of Mexico and the US and Chihuahua, Texas, and New Mexico. A preacher from Juárez looks south and admits he has not been in Juárez in a year because of the violence.

"Brown Eyed Girl" purrs from the speakers.

Two dozen ducks fly over.

Michael Jackson tells the tale of "Billie Jean."

Red, yellow and pink zinnias listen by the stucco wall. A winch hangs down from an unfinished arch flanked by concrete columns. El Pastor talks of his recurrent dream: he is in the Coliseum in Rome fighting the lions for his faith. He thinks that he will be there in a year or two. He has this sense that he will visit Rome and step into the arena and feel his dream of years become a moment. It will happen, he says. And then he laughs.

There is this edge in his talk, a fine sharp line between what he believes with all his heart and how he knows the world sees what he believes with all his heart. He knows he will be in Rome in the arena and he knows this sounds foolish to others and so he laughs at himself before they can. His God has made him comfortable with both his faith and the foolishness of his faith. He can be mocked so long as he is allowed to believe.

He takes the mike and booms out his own birthday sermon to his guests, about how he is the product of a single sperm out of hundreds of millions launched and this sperm succeeded—POW!—and his life came tumbling down the years and here he is. The smoke drifts across him and he stands there in his black shoes and pants and coat and shirt— the costume he created when he heard the call and became

El Pastor—and amens arise from his guests and some bow their heads. Off to the side, a guitar player waits for his moment.

Everything in his life is here—wife, children, grandchildren, nieces, nephews, friends, and relics of his former life on the streets. The asylum is across that border, miles away in Juárez, but it is also here because that is his work and his work gathers the people and tonight the people are here to celebrate his birthday because of his work. And this is a moment in the flash of life, that thing that passes so quickly and then you go into the hole in the ground and El Pastor is buoyant and morose at the same moment. He is driving down a barrio street before the party and he says suddenly "life is a line drawn in water, it's there and then it is suddenly gone," and this time he does not laugh.

The night slowly comes down, the city lights flicker, the guitar player sings

You left me alone
With the stars

and a child walks through the door holding a pink balloon, cuts through the blue smoke coming off the grills, and the light comes on and beams out of the half-finished arch and the guitar player apologizes and explains he normally plays rhythm but the lead guitar was not allowed to cross the bridge and so then nothing need be said since everyone deals with the bridge and the rules and the changing rules and he sings

For you I stop thinking of the sea
For you I stop thinking of the sky

and the man wears black and is thickset and has a fine tenor and the patron, the man who brought him from Juárez, watches the performance like a hawk because he is a man used to getting what he wants and he slaps his thigh to the beat and never smiles because he was once in the life and now he is not but the habit of being wary and being exact and being in charge can never leave him and El Pastor moves from person to person, and table to table, and he laughs and beams, and yet somewhere behind his eyes lurks the fatigue because every day and into the night he must be this person he invented, El Pastor. He must tend to the crazy people and he must find money and the work never ends and the singer dedicates a song to a man dressed head to toe in black, the patron who has brought him across the river to his patio, a man whose past trails behind in the city and this past both stalks him and protects him because he has been and still is someone who reeks of power and so the singer says

Because of you my life is hell

and the drum machine kicks in again and he sings

I am coming here to open up my heart

and the crowd is thinning now, the party beginning to ebb and so the singer goes into the songs that are for him and now for the guests and he has written a song about Juárez, "March for Unity in Juárez," and he strums the guitar and

There is no evil that can conquer your heart

and later he says "I was born in the USA but I am from Juárez."

Migrations

She runs a newspaper on the US side of the line and says she feels safe and that the violence stays in Mexico. This is the way we survive—by keeping some distance between the killings and our sense of self. But she admits she no longer drives in Mexico at night. She no longer goes to the party spots in the red-light zone either. There are carjackings. And then she drifts off.

She says the previous editor of the border-town paper never covered any violence in Mexico. He was afraid.

So you see, she says, there have been some good changes.

The local restaurant is full of refugees from the other side, like most border towns these days.

I hear the woman's voice, and she is sensible, and it matters not at all to me.

She says, "What has spilled over is dread."

I have two strong desires. To settle down. And to leave.

I have never been a migrant. I have never had to leave a place against my will nor have I ever been driven out by want. The stories I hear from the wayfarers on the line could never fall from my lips. I never take a risk that is even remotely equal to the dangers they face. My country has never treated me as trash and my country has never refused to protect me.

My ancestors went off to find a new country. The Mexicans flee home.

I know my way is rough and steep
Yet beauteous fields lie just before me
Where God's redeemed their vigils keep

*   *   *

I get up at two thirty a.m. and work. Coffee begins to leave my life as the miles increase. The sky is overcast, the humidity chokes. I can feel a storm threat bobbing and weaving in the still air. I move through a drizzle. Black hawks call out but I cannot see them, the deer now are hidden by the towering Johnson grass, the gray hawks invisible to me.

In ten miles, I see some javelinas. But that is enough. I no longer look for things. I no longer tally. If nothing happens, that is almost more than I can absorb. The movement of water across rock fills me. The first flowers from the monsoon stud the land with blue and orange.

Now I suddenly catch scents from childhood, and these scents trigger memories. I am with my mother wading through lilies of the valley, or planting green beans in hills. The chickens splayed on crushed ice in the market on 79th Street in Chicago, the acid smell of rotting apples under the trees in the orchard.

The pack now weighs twenty pounds and yet this is not enough.

I crave the weight.

I sit for hours staring at birds. I have turned off music in the house. I cringe when I hear a human voice and move off and go into a thicket until the voices move on.

At first I think about escape, how I will flee the dullness that seems to be taking me down and return to the sense of wonder that filled my three-year-old eyes and that I can now suddenly recall for the first time in a year. I stop reading magazines. I do not watch television. I turn off the radio. I read old books and field guides. My current events become no more recent than the Pleistocene.

In the gray light a doe crosses the road, each step is as light as a cat's. She does not see me and I begin to feel like I belong and am getting closer to what I am joining.

Juárez

The room has no windows. Fluorescent lights hum overhead, the lawyer sits at the end of the conference table, the man and his nephew speak of what has become of their lives and how they came to have so many dead.

He is a baker, his father too was a baker, so were his brothers bakers. Now four brothers are dead, the sister also, a nephew, friends of the family. All dead. All killed by the Mexican army.

Julio Cesar Reyes Salazar is murdered in November 2009. His mother, Josefina, is slaughtered in January 2010. Ruben Reyes Salazar is killed August 8, 2010. Maria Magdalena Reyes Salazar goes down February 7, 2011, along with Elias Reyes Salazar and Ornelias de Reyes. Family associates in the protests die also—Marisela Escobeda, December 16, 2010, Armando Villareal, March 23, 2008, Dr. Manuel Arroyo Galvan, May 29, 2009. They seem to die the same way—by bullets fired into their heads.

The baker says there was this day when the surviving members of his family were in downtown Ciudad Juárez. When they got home to their village on the outskirts of the city their house had been burned and the graves of their recent dead desecrated. The man says the cross over his sister's grave was uprooted that day and still sits in front of the army barracks leaning against a wall. Bodies were dug up.

Thirty-three of his family members go to Mexico City and ask the United Nations for protection from their own nation. Their plea is denied.

He is a man around forty and now is seeking safety in the US. He is homeless and should he win, he will be marooned here.

I ask him how much longer does this killing go on.

He says, "At least ten more years."

I'm going there to see my mother
She said she'd meet me when I come
I'm only going over Jordan
I'm only going over home

Marisol Valles became Joan of Arc one December day when she needed a job. She was twenty, a single mother, and then the position of police chief fell vacant in Praxedis G. Guerrero near Juárez following the beheading of the top cop. The mayor picked her because he thought she'd threaten no one. The town was the same place the baker hailed from. It sported a murder rate as high as 2,000 per 100,000 residents. It was likely the most lethal place to live on Earth.

She announced she would have three deputies, all women, and none of them would carry guns, and none of them would look into drug cases nor arrest anyone. Marisol was in school studying criminology which led her to focus on community policing.

The world press rushed in and said a young girl was taking on the drug organizations in a nation where the men had failed or lost their nerve. Marisol Valles became famous all over the world. By spring, she fled to the US to save her life.

At the same time that Marisol assumed her police position, a woman in a neighboring town became a chief also. But she was somewhat older and darker than Marisol. The press

ignored her. She was kidnapped within weeks and nothing
more has ever been heard of her.

I want to wear a crown of glory
When I get home to that good land
I want to shout salvation's story
In concert with the blood-washed band

I'm going there to meet my Savior
To sing his praise forevermore
I'm only going over Jordan
I'm only going over home

El Pastor

The tiles in the clinic are slightly off-white. Outside on the patio, the crazy people mill around in the noonday heat. There is very little shade. Some sit on the ground and stare off into space. Others howl and growl. The air is rich with sounds.

On the wall is a painting of a man sitting on a pile of trash in a Juárez alley. He is flanked by two garbage cans. Christ kneels to tend to him. The man has tattered jeans, a torn red shirt. His hair is scruffy as is his beard. He is the man who founded the asylum, the man who loves to eat a stack of beefsteaks. The painting captures the moment he was saved and suggests what he was saved from—a life on the streets of Juárez as an addict.

God is part of his explanation for all the pain that once flooded his life and all the pain that now inhabits his asylum. There is a sense of end-time floating over Juárez, a feeling that the killing has reached such a fever pitch that it must have some meaning and just might be the fury of the wrath of God.

It cannot be explained as simply a drug war. Nor can it be explained as simply caused by poverty or corrupt police or a brutal military or thieving politicians. These elements have always been part of the fabric of life here.

So God is invoked.
The real fear is not the killing.
It is that the killing might mean nothing at all.

The Cranes

There is that Siberian crane who lived eighty-three years in captivity and fathered chicks at seventy-eight. In China, cranes came to symbolize longevity and some thought they must live centuries. In Japan, Yorimoto in the twelfth century put paper bands on cranes. The stories say these birds with bands were found for centuries. People started to think cranes might live a thousand years.

Cranes mate for life and people noticed this fact and wove crane images into their weddings and dreams. Some thought they carried the souls of dead warriors into heaven as rewards for valor.

I stand by the marsh, sun on my face and the cranes are out there on the wet ground, strutting, making that talk, alive to the moment and to the next moment and I am in a store and in that line and the man's hat says veteran of one of those wars and he's hobbling and the young woman has no hips but lots of tattoos in the line ahead of me and she's clutching that big bottle of wine and later in the parking lot I see her unwind that motorcycle, she's leaning forward, the spread-eagle blue design riding over her ass, summer is over, night comes down, the light fading and people hardly notice the coming of the stars.

And there is this matter of the cranes dancing.

Jericho

Jericho was the first place to test the Israelites after they had wandered in the wilderness for forty years. There was the issue of walls. Also of spies and traitors. And genocide since every living thing—save the family of the whore—was put to the sword. So it is written.

A homeless poverty-stricken people wanders for decades, enters Canaan, makes music, the walls fall down.

And then everyone dies.

The oldest staircase in the world is here.

So too, the oldest wall.

Later—there is always later—Jesus Christ faced his temptation near Jericho and

Then was Jesus led up of the Spirit into the wilderness to be tempted of the devil. And when he had fasted forty days and forty nights, afterwards he was hungry. And when the tempter came to him, he said, If thou be the Son of God, command that these stones be made bread. But he answered and said, It is written, Man shall not live by bread alone, but by every word that proceedeth out of the mouth of God. (Matt. 4: 1–4)

Peque on Ice

Juan Carlos Navarro came up five blocks from the line. He was twenty-one when he was found wrapped in a blanket just across the fence in Nogales, Sonora. The body showed signs of torture. The people in his barrio said he crossed over with a friend who had some problems with bad guys to see if he could help. The friend has not been seen since.

He was called Peque, Little Guy. A few years earlier, he'd been busted for helping to load some marijuana, but since then, there had been no reported incidents. He lived with his ailing mother, he was an expectant father, and he was going to junior college.

The day is sunny, a pause within the storms of the summer monsoon. The two plainclothes agents stand by the unmarked truck. They are on the prowl for dope runners who course through the mountains near Nogales.

Ah, yeah, that kid in Nogales, one says, nobody's going to make a fuss over his killing, the word is he got in with some bad people.

Hummingbirds swirl around them, a pair of ravens croak in the cottonwood by the creek. On December 14, 2010, Border Patrol agent Brian Terry was gunned down when his SWAT team ran into armed Mexicans some miles north of the line. Turned out the Mexicans were fully armed with guns supplied by the ATF in a sting called Operation Fast and Furious, yet no one wants to talk about the unanswered questions in that killing.

The agents wear their shirts outside their pants to cover their guns. Nogales, Arizona, where Peque came up has about twenty thousand people. Nogales had its first killing in three years—an ex-cop killed his estranged wife.

The agents shuffle their feet in the dirt and inhale the fresh air after the storm. The ground is wet, the dust settled, the grass greening during a brief interlude in years of drought. They mutter about politicians inventing a fuss over border violence, they mumble about agency corruption in various sectors on the US side, and they dismiss the murder of Peque out of hand. He got in with some bad business.

People in Peque's neighborhood are holding car washes to pay for his cremation—at the moment he is still on ice. The girl who speaks to the press for the family says she wants everyone to understand that no one is seeking vengeance, that no one wants any more violence. On the border this translates as: Don't kill us too, we will not talk to the authorities.

For ten years or more, the counties on the US side of the border have seen crime decline. El Paso is rated about the safest city of its size in the United States. Neighboring Ciudad Juárez is possibly the most violent city on earth. In 2010, more than three thousand people were murdered in Juárez. In El Paso, five people were murdered—two of them were murder/suicides. Such facts have no place in the border discussions of many US politicians.

Falcon Lake

When the incident with David Hartley occurs on September 30, 2010, Governor Rick Perry of Texas says, "This is a tragedy. It is a result of many years of disregard for the people along that border, and the security of the border. We've been telling this administration, and administrations before, for years, that there is not enough support, there's not enough boots on the ground, there's not enough technology in place—aviation assets—to protect the citizens of the United States—and Mexico for that matter. And now we're beginning to see concrete evidence of that failure to secure the border, when American citizens, an innocent American citizen who was down there strictly on a historical trip to take a picture of the old church at Guerrero, is murdered on Lake Falcon.... Any one who says anything other than this was pirates or just criminal element [*sic*] out on that lake that killed an innocent American—there is nothing there. We've asked all the right questions. Our sheriff has asked the right questions. Anyone who is trying to deflect off of what this actually is ought to be ashamed of themselves."

Sheriff Sigifredo Gonzalez Jr. of Zapata County handles the Hartley case and believes Tiffany's account almost instantly. He sees the border as dangerous, with violence slopping over the line. "If smugglers can bring a hundred people or 2,000 pounds of marijuana into the United States, how simple would it be to bring terrorists into this country, or a suitcase loaded with a dirty bomb?" Gonzalez told the *Washington Times* in 2005. "I am very surprised it hasn't already happened." He never asks Tiffany to take a polygraph. He says there was no need.

* * *

Twice, I see small birds chase three whistling ducks from the east end of the refuge. The ducks flee across the dirt road as the little birds pursue them up the hill and into the mesquite slopes. Black hawks call in early morning, the keening sound a knife through the early light. Later, I spot one as it lands on a bare perch just east of the heron rookery. The hawk stares at me, gives its call, ruffles its wings, and then, settles in.

A green and yellow vireo, a rare Mexican visitor, has been sighted. The wildlife refuge is thronged with people. They look very grim. Their faces display the desperate need of all trophy hunters. The men vary—some with cautious, granola faces, some with whiskey written in their gaze. The women all seem similar and scentless.

The sky is overcast until around ten a.m. I make 12.2 miles in under four hours with three liters in the pack. I am numbers now, my world a green treadmill and I think if I note simple unadorned facts I will finally belong to a world.

* * *

In the five years before the Hartleys visit Falcon Lake, more than two hundred Americans are murdered in Mexico without much outcry from the US government. But there is something about David Hartley that makes his case different—he is white. The Peques get tortured and murdered without much talk.

The reported attack on David Hartley happens between six and eight miles into Mexico, a nation he illegally entered.

He has become the poster child for violence spilling across the border and his widow a spokesperson for the issue. She feels this is a mission, something God intended for her.

* * *

There is twilight blue, lichen, paprika, green apple, magma, cone red, moss green, iron gray, graphite, ocean, nettle pewter, beet juice, black steel, chili pepper, and ivy green. The rains have come, chiggers ride my legs, the air is heavy, tepid, the smell of a swamp. The deer become invisible as the grass shoots up. The herons have clearly moved on, the rookery is closed for the year.

Iris, clover, meteorite, cayenne, dusk blue, tundra, amethyst, aquamarine, midnight storm.

There is a big wind after midnight but no rain falls. I find broken limbs across the road and trails.

Tuolomne green, scarlet, bluebird, terracotta, Pacific.

I walk and walk. I never want to stop. I avoid all people.

I dream packs and the colors of packs.

Fern.

* * *

In the spring of 2010, there are incidents on Falcon Lake. The sheriff reports that boaters seeking largemouth bass were approached three times by Mexicans seeking money near Zapata. Almost all of the lake falls on the Mexican side and Americans fishing go where the bass are. For decades the lake has boasted world-class fishing and been free of serious incidents.

The Hartleys have been living for two years in Reynosa,

the Mexican city facing McAllen. David Hartley works for an oil company, Calfrac Well Services. Earlier he'd been posted to Siberia, a tour his wife skipped. They are regular church-goers and have made church-sponsored visits to Kenya and Juárez. That spring, they visit San Antonio to hear Dave Ramsey, a debt guru, evangelical Christian and onetime bankrupt, who wars against spending more than you make. That June they buy two Sea-Doos, jet skis that run well over ten thousand dollars each.

They have experienced some problems in Reynosa as violence begins exploding in Mexico after Felipe Calderón assumes the presidency in December 2006. David is robbed by local police and beaten. In September 2009 they have to suddenly move from their house in Reynosa because their landlord is having problems with a drug cartel. They stay in McAllen for a spell, but then find another house in Reynosa.

They visit Falcon Lake in August and ski for three or four hours. Later, after the incident, Tiffany says on television that during that visit they talked to Border Patrol agents about the danger of being on the lake and were told their jet skis could easily outrun any bad guys. Their Sea-Doos can go from zero to thirty in 1.7 seconds, and easily hit 75 mph.

Tiffany Hartley said she and her husband knew of the robberies, but since nothing had happened on the lake for months they were not worried. She also said she and her husband had lived in Reynosa with "no fear." In fact, she said No Fear was the family motto for David and her. She also said her husband sheltered her from what was going on in the city.

By February 2010, the US Consulate in Reynosa shut down for a spell due to gun battles. In March two reporters were kidnapped and a third reporter died, the government said from an embolism but those who saw the corpse said he had been badly beaten. During a three-week period in February and March 2010, this city of half a million had two hundred murders. By August, authorities began to discover mass graves about ninety miles south of Reynosa. By fall, a leader of the ruling party called the city a war zone.

* * *

Two deer move like ghosts on the ridge in the rain, the tan hides melting into the gray sky. The air sags with moisture, no one else is out and I hear my footsteps crunch on the earth, hear the cry of a hawk. I see the doe and young buck twice in the refuge, once browsing in the ciénaga, later in the meadow of Johnson grass near the abandoned railroad bed. The young buck has the nubbins of horns beginning but still tries to suck off the doe, which pushes him aside. They look like a tapestry in the gray light.

I leave the pack behind and walk eleven miles in the rain. The world feels fresh and I am the only inhabitant of this fresh world. I have had this sensation sometimes, when running trails in mountains, of being cut loose from people and laws and clocks and bound only by the culture of the things around me on the mountainside.

Once I leave my house before dawn and drive to the base of the mountain. I start running in the gray light and a faint rain falls on my body. I wear shorts and a T-shirt. The trail is steep and strewn with rocks. About an hour into the run a buck with a big rack explodes from the manzanita. Thunder begins to roll off the peak and I keep climbing and then clouds brush against me and I feel the hair on my neck rise and suddenly there is lightning above, to my side and below me and I move inside the rain and cloud and electrical surges and I am the tallest thing in the desert scrub on the slope. When I reach the top, I look down at the swirling storm, then turn and run through it again. When I finally get down and reach my parked car by the road it is like trading life for death.

Falcon Lake

The Hartleys get on their expensive new jet skis and roar up an old channel. They are living upriver at McAllen/Reynosa and they go to a church that tells them God is on their side and believes in love and prosperity and they go to a debt counseling program and they spend a lot of money on the jet skis and come to Falcon Lake when the job ends in Reynosa or when jobs vanish from their lives—it is never really clear—but they come with debts it seems and new machines they love and she says it is about history, all about history, that David Hartley devours the past, and now as the dead town rises from the waters he must see it before he leaves the region in a few days for other states or countries where he can make his living, and get on with life and it is early in the afternoon, still September hot on the border, and they are skimming across Falcon Lake, a body of water that in the main is a narrow snake, but they are heading up the old river channel that winds eight miles into Mexico to the village rising from the receding waters, and on the banks they see scrub, a neotropical landscape that at first says desert and then looks too rich and green for the word, a place of thorns and trees and grass and brown earth where men huddle in fishing camps and try to wring a living from the impounded waters and anis stand on drowned limbs, black, the bills grooved, the whole scene looks off, but just slightly off, and has that feel of something from the deep south and other, that whisper of lushness masked by burning sun and blue sky and thorns and there are rumors in the air of bandits and men with guns and drugs moving across the lake at will, talk of danger but the Hartleys ignore these warnings and so does everyone else on the lake, all the bass fishermen, all the Mexicans netting fish for market, all the drug guys seeking to eke out some money by moving a load, everyone forgets about these stories because the reports fail to mesh with the everyday feel and experience of the lake and so they are out there, on their skis, machines that accelerate like motorcycles and the wind in their faces, the air, fresh water, and sunshine, broomtails of spray behind them, the roar of the engines deafening, on a lake of bass fishermen and dope runners they are the only people in a hurry, the only people creating a great wake and they come out of the inlet with the public launch ramp, then angle over toward the drowned river, soon fly past the buoys marking the international boundary and now they are in Mexico and they don't give it a thought, no one does, they feel the vibration, the hum of the throttle in their hand, the ease as the machine flies on top of the water, they are free, they are young, they are leaving an old home for a new home, they are an open book and all these pages have yet to be written, perhaps they will have children, move to a foreign country, maybe learn a language or two, make new friends, it is all there, ready and waiting.

Beneath their skis lurk huge bass and they are caught and re-caught because the ethic of the lake is to almost always release bass, the breeding females, they are the deep rhythm of the lake where fish live and die, and men come to catch them in an effort to forget their lives, their work, and their women. But this is not on the mind of David Hartley nor is it probably on the mind of Tiffany Hartley.

All we know is that they fly across the lake on new jet skis and go up a river to see a drowned village and that he never comes back. After that moment, he is transformed and his body and blood become things used by others—by politicians to decry violence on the border, by Tiffany Hartley to use as her credentials for saying we must send men and guns to the border for our security. David Hartley vanishes and leaves no body and yet in death he looms over the lake.

I want to blast a shofar, a ram's horn, march seven times round Falcon Lake and see what tumbles down, maybe a dam, maybe a border, maybe some lies and liars. The rocks will bang and roll, the earth shake, there will be blood in the sky and on the ground, birds will scream in the night, the buildings will be no more, the dying will be vast and forests will move, beasts will storm north and south, the boundaries will be stomped into dust, and the river is dying and the temperatures rising and there are too many dead to count.

He becomes a living thing though he is believed dead. His body becomes a sacred quest on the part of his wife and family. She says she just wants the body back, she is not interested in revenge. And so the dead man who lacks a body becomes a holy relic, a thing that must be found in order for the family to have peace, a thing that must be found in order for the United States to feel some semblance of justice, a thing of flesh and bone and blood that now transcends nations and becomes larger than anything that has ever crossed Falcon Lake or swum in its waters.

I step out on the plaza and it is dead quiet. Once the line ran just north of here and then the line moved just south of here and this is seldom remembered since the belief now is that lines are forever and are made into walls and maybe I think I should get a shofar and prance seven times up and down the wall blowing and it will come tumbling down.

———

The wall stands and grows and everyone believes that the wall stands.

The agents stand and grow and everyone believes that the agents stand.

The dead shuffle by, mile after mile of the dead and no one believes in the dead and they are hardly spoken of and soon they will not only never have lived, they will never have died.

The Cranes

I am told I cannot go up into the sky but I lift my head when I hear the cranes.

I am two, maybe younger, crawling through the dirt between the rows of beans and tomatoes in the garden. I see a woman's legs up ahead, she is bending and then straightening up, pinching things here, cutting there, moving, working, glancing back at me crawling. There is a huge spiked caterpillar on a tomato vine, and there is a sweet smell off the earth, not sour, no, not sour, sweet as everyone knows who has gotten down and sucked off the soil, the dirt crumbling between my tiny fingers, and later I think, hey, maybe that is when I began my lust for life that others told me spelled death. There is this morning, I suck up dirt, a woman moves down the row, cutting here, picking there, the earth rampant, the plants teeming, the harvest a gleam but we all know it is coming, and the blue sky echoes the calls of birds.

There was a moment years later as November slammed down on my life like a jail sentence when I stood outside on a moonless night and heard Canadian geese honking overhead as they fled south and left me marooned in winter.

My heart ached.

Now I hear cranes overhead following the river and that pain and yearning returns.

Jericho

Jericho is way below sea level but it does not drown. That is not part of God's plan. Jericho will not be preserved beneath the waters. Jericho will die by the sword, and all the stones and walls will fall.

> And it shall come to pass, that when they make a long blast with the ram's horn, and when ye hear the sound of the trumpet, all the people shall shout with a great shout; and the wall of the city shall fall down flat, and the people shall ascend up every man straight before him. And Joshua the son of Nun called the priests, and said unto them, Take up the ark of the covenant, and let seven priests bear seven trumpets of rams' horns before the ark of the LORD. And he said unto the people, Pass on, and compass the city, and let him that is armed pass on before the ark of the LORD. (Josh. 6.5–6.7)

Jericho has messages hidden in its death. For thousands of years holy men ring these messages like bells and this din falls on the ears of man. The stories are about the glory of God and the frailty of walls and about whores and traitors and how all this is a very fine thing if you look at it correctly.

*   *   *

*Overcast, 80 degrees, humid. I load the pack up with more
water and now I carry at least twenty-five pounds. I do ten
miles and it feels better than five miles without a pack back
when I began this foolishness. I want to move with forty-five
pounds forever, with a small tarp shelter, the bag and stove,
water and food, binoculars and books, a water filter, clothes.
Yes, move with forty-five pounds forever, and have my body
ready for the work. I think of walking across the state even
though I no longer believe in states. I think of walking the di-
vide from Canada to Mexico even though I no longer believe
in countries.*

I feel balance leaving me.

*If I hear a human voice, it sounds like an explosion, all
the tones harsh and off-key.*

I begin to understand why the game beats away.

*For the first time in years I begin to plan. I study maps
and consider a route that will swallow days and forty or fifty
miles. I calculate how much gear I will need to never come
back.*

Seeing the stars.

Sleeping on the ground.

The night winds rustling through the brush soothe me.

Falcon Lake

The den is full of trophies of the outdoors. A deer head, a cluster of antlers on top of a shelf. The man has been fishing Falcon Lake for over thirty years, almost always in Mexican waters. He says he has never kept a fish. The lake is fabled for having monsters but it is a catch-and-release kind of place.

In all those years of fishing he's never had a lick of trouble from the Mexicans and he wants to keep it that way. Tamaulipas, the state across from Falcon Lake, is having a blood bath. The Gulf Cartel is busy fighting its former colleagues, the Zetas. And the Mexican army pitches in and kills wholesale also.

The area just across the lake is considered Zeta turf. The Zetas, a band of killers that originally was a special anti-drug unit in the nineties and then decided to kill for a drug organization, given the better pay, decided after a while to take over from their new bosses, the Gulf Cartel, and that among other things led to the current slaughter.

The man does not wish for the Zetas to interfere with his bass fishing.

On September 30, he got up early and went out on the lake with his wife. In the early afternoon, as he recalls, he came back to the public ramp, left his wife in the boat and went to fetch his trailer and truck.

He found a guy on the ramp having trouble getting two new Sea-Doos off his trailer. The guy was extremely pleasant and they chatted and then after about ten or twelve minutes, the man who'd been fishing all morning left with his wife.

Later, he heard about the shooting. When he saw a picture of the surviving Sea-Doo in the paper, he knew it was one of the two he saw.

He's never talked about that moment to authorities.

There was one other thing he recalls. During the ten or twelve minutes he was at the ramp loading his boat and David Hartley was at the ramp trying to unload his Sea-Doos, the man never saw anyone else.

He never knew Tiffany Hartley was along.

There is really nothing at the ramp except an area for parking boat trailers and trucks. There are no businesses, no buildings. Just desert scrub.

El Sicario

The white dog hunts rats under a moonless sky in the hour before dawn. Rank odors rise off the flowerbeds and the pumpkin vine stalks, shrubs, and trees. I can barely shake the airports out of my body and still can hear the soft lapping of the Adriatic against the Lido. That dawn I stand on the sand and speak into the camera about Ciudad Juárez while women walk by in tight pants with expensive hair and navigate the stone steps with stiletto heels. The Hotel Excelsior hums with film people and everyone talks on phones or shoots footage of the grayness coming off the sea.

The man recording me asks if Juárez is safe, can he visit for two days for his Italian newspaper and why is it so violent there and what is the social meaning of all the dead people. I have had a twenty-hour flight and almost no sleep. Not even the water taxi threading through Murano broke my coma.

Across the lagoon is Venice with the cathedral stuffed with loot from Byzantium that the locals stole when the imperial city plundered the Mediterranean. This era of greed has smeared locals with a garish taste that lingers even after Napoleon retired the legends of the doges and Venice sank into a bog of irrelevance. The Murano glass retains this appetite for violent color despite it now being a financial toy of the Chinese. And down the coast at Split in Croatia, Diocletian's Palace has survived the centuries thanks to squatters carving out apartments and shopkeepers fashioning an urban mall.

Diocletian was the last man to try and save Rome from the new Christian God and a genius at torturing human life with bureaucracy. He found an empire that could not pay its bills, revised taxes, created new zones and tiers of power and returned to the Illyrian coast of his childhood, threw up his palace and sank into his dreams.

Nothing here is within my reach. Everything costs a lot and I have nothing. The film is an accident. I was in New Orleans and drinking wine and murder. Something about the city has tugged at me since childhood when I walked the French Market with my aunt. We were going to make a movie about wet air, crumbled housing, killings, police and the feel of something beyond our words.

I was staying in a cheap motel run by subcontinent Indians, some with caste marks on their foreheads. The other guests were crews rebuilding the bones of the destroyed city. Or illegal Mexicans packed each night in rooms like livestock and then sent out each day to tear out mold-ridden walls. The Mexicans all coughed from their work and kept grills outside their rooms where they made carne asada. Across the parking lot was a twenty-four-hour bar that featured lounge music, a temple to Frank Sinatra's classic albums of the late fifties and this playlist was salted with torch songs from the forties. The bartender was a woman from Croatia who smiled at the regulars and gave them an acre of cleavage with their drinks. Late at night, the place hummed and yet slept. There were no loud voices, just a visit to a dream that had never really happened, a place of babes and guys and dolls and mixed drinks in glasses with very slender stems.

I mentioned the sicario to my friend, the director, and by July, we were looking for the right room. We hit motel after motel but the sicario found them all wanting. He had special needs for his security, needs he did not tell us because he saw us as fools who knew nothing of his life. Finally, we found a space—Room 164—that he insisted upon. Only days later we learned it was a room that he rented for torturing his kidnap victims. The filming itself was to be a simple matter. The sicario would wear a veil—he had a $250,000 contract on his head, moved constantly, and did not like his face shown around. We would get enough film for maybe six minutes of vignettes for a grander project we had in mind.

And then he began speaking and spoke for days without a stumble, spoke of his life, of his work, of power, of terror and finally of God. There was nothing to be done but let him have his way. He became a movie and we became witnesses to his movie.

And the film premieres in the Venice Festival, the oldest such gathering in the world, a thing launched in 1943 when Mussolini still ruled, though his name has been erased now and everything is film and theory and women in tight clothes with high heels on the Lido. Film has homages to its gods, directors, but no real past. The world and its wounds are simply a pantry of images to be plucked, rearranged and admired. Thomas Mann decided to have his *Death in Venice* here, and there was a time when the great doge himself lived on his barrier island of sand.

The interview finally ends. I sip espresso and watch people hurrying past to various showings at the neighboring Movie Village. During the following press conference, a critic asks me why I made such a film. I do not realize until later he thinks the film is a theatrical invention—I learn it has been posted as a fictional thing. I tell the critic I did not travel to Venice to give him pleasure.

*   *   *

He sits in the chair in the room with the red sofa. The air conditioning is off and he is very hot under his black veil. Sometimes he weeps, but now he is calm. He likes this room for the memories. For three days, he tortured the man in the bathroom. Then the man was taken back across the river and handed off to other men. The family paid but the man was likely killed. This is the custom.

He thinks he once worked for Satan and that the government of Juárez, the police of Juárez, the politicians of Juárez, the army patrolling Juárez, the press reporting Juárez, the sicarios cruising Juárez, that all of these elements live in an illusion and that the city itself is nothing but a machine of death that pumps money into the only reality, the drug world. He begins sketching, and then he starts weeping as he draws a circle of the family of man and the love of God and muffled cries come through his black veil.

He keeps remembering.

All resources will now be shared at the point of a gun.

All streets will offer equal safety.

The lamb will now lie down with the lion.

And be eaten.

In room 164, the man in the veil keeps remembering assignments.

He cannot seem to stop drawing.

There is a house that has an attached garage. He sketches five dead in the house. And in the corner of the patio, he buries another fifteen. He writes the words FBI and DEA and draws an arrow to this bone yard. Some of the agencies' informants now sleep here.

He never looks up.

He is a veil, a sketchbook and a pen that never tires.

El Pastor

El Pastor's painting shows a doll hanging from a wire in a Juárez neighborhood of abandoned houses. People have fled because of the violence and because of the poverty. The houses are ruins with pipes and wires ripped out. The doll is unexplained.

So he paints a canvas: Satan overlooks the ruins, the doll hangs in a perfect blue sky, the moon seems to be rising as a skull, the Mexican flag waves. There is a broken basketball hoop with the net half hanging. One game is over.

A filmmaker has been living in the crazy place of El Pastor. He is struck by the rhythms of the days and nights. And he notices that the inmates run the asylum.

The crazy place is a place of love and he worries about catching this fact on film because the love is in small gestures and little moments and the murder of the city is gunshots and the flashing lights of police and the scream of ambulances rushing to a kill site.

Falcon Lake

Doug Fetts has fished Falcon Lake for six years. He is a guide, the fee here runs $400 a day. Before that he was on the pro bass tournament circuit. Now he moves about the lake in a fifty-thousand-dollar bass boat. Business took a hard hit after David Hartley vanished. Clients were afraid to go on the water. Or their wives were afraid to let them go fishing.

Fetts says, "Over that ridge, they wiped out a camp."

By "they," he means the Mexican army and by "camp" he means a bunch of Zetas. The organization has become a shorthand here for bad people on the Mexican side of the lake.

Doug steers his boat miles into Mexico. He is here pretty much every day. When the television people showed up after the Hartley incident Doug took them out.

Now he is running me eight miles into Mexico to Guerrero Viejo, the old town drowned by the lake that the Hartleys wanted to visit.

Groove-billed anis rest on drowned trees. A great blue heron flies overhead. A half dozen pangas are pulled up on the bank and Doug slows.

"They look like Zetas," he allows.

I glance at them through binoculars and they look like poor guys who catch fish for a living.

Doug thinks the real reason for the incidents of robbery last year was simply that some of the guys moving drugs across the lake got marooned because of the military sweeps and were hungry. They'd come up to boats asking for a Coke or some food.

The trick is to not get cornered in some small backwater by guys in pangas. Their fishing boats can barely crack twenty miles an hour, Doug's bass boat can hit sixty.

* * *

Two black-bellied whistling ducks fly by shortly after dawn.

There has been a riot in the prison in Juárez and the official count is at least seventeen dead. I learn later that the dead were more than forty but this is never reported in the media.

The fact that I know the father of a guy in there walks the creek with me.

I see three common black hawks and one immature zone tail. I sweat a lot, and go ten miles with twenty-five pounds in the pack. I have crossed from fatigue into some dreamland where my limited body can do just enough to sustain my fantasies.

Huge thunderheads begin to form off the peaks before noon.

The sky promises violence.

I think of walking through the rain and lightning of a summer night and then the sweet air after the storm moves on and the sound of rising water tumbling down the canyons.

I think of the dead in Juárez.

I stare at a blue grosbeak on a fence post by the road.

There is a video of the killing in the prison—two gangs normally kept separate get at each other's throats. In the security video, the guards let gang members into the unit of the other gang, give them guns and then the armed men go into the cellblocks and kill and kill and kill. It is organized. Later, the gang leader of the killers gives up three of his guys who are already serving long sentences for murder, men who can suffer no additional penalty. The state solves the crime it sponsored.

A garter snake races by my foot.

The slow wingbeat of a great blue heron passes over my shadow.

In Texas a servicemen's organization and a labor union put out a study that blames illegal Mexicans for low wages, unemployment, bad health and weakened national security. Operation Wetback is seen by many as a great success because it made Mexicans move.

When the project ended nothing really changed except the talk of fear since the government said the problem was now solved, that its deportation of eighty thousand had scared another million into fleeing south of the river, and that the nation was secure. It did issue about four hundred thousand permits a year for farm workers so that payment of a living wage could be avoided. Everything was fine until it was no longer fine. As Mexico's economy soured in the 1980s and the lust for cheap wages intoxicated American employers, the flow of illegal Mexican labor resumed and so did the cries of invasion, health problems and the erosion of national security.

A coyote moves off slowly and throws a backward glance at me that is as light as a feather.

The bees seize the hummingbird feeders and I cannot sit outside because of their aggression. Here, they are all crossed with African invaders.

The border moves, the lies shift and change and come again. The violence is always coming from the south except that it mainly seems to come from the north.

I walk serenely. I know that facts do not matter on the border.

Birds matter. Trees matter. The moon crossing the night sky matters.

One night at about 1:30 a.m. there are bursts of automatic gunfire down along the creek. The coyotes do not howl but the owls hoot near dawn.

The Mexicans continue to move, the agents continue to plan.

The border is the place that has broken me. And I know as I walk the hills and the hawks cry out in the day and the owls hoot in the night, the border is the place that will mend me.

Or nothing and no place will.

A gray hawk calls.

Roma was the head of navigation for steamboats on the river and they pulled below the bluff where the old city still sits. Now it is a beaten border town with a core of ancient brick buildings, most of them vacant. One schoolteacher figures about a third of the parents deal drugs. The only thing certain is that there is not much money around Roma and drugs mean money and risk. Across the river is Ciudad Miguel Alemán. In April 2011, armed men entered the town and burned the police station and other buildings including a Ford dealership. They were said to be Zetas.

It's a hundred and four and a row of pickup trucks is parked on the Mexican shore of the river as people come down to the water to cool off. The town itself feels dead. The usual border constellation of pharmacies and dental offices are empty. No one comes here now.

A tienda sells large statues of Santa Muerte, a new object of devotion for the poor and a favorite of people in the drug industry. One has the bony saint riding a Harley Davidson.

The café bakes with the air stirred by a few fans. When I ask for a beer, the owner leaves to go buy a few cans.

Liz Rogers is a federal defense attorney in Alpine, Texas, the town facing the emptiness of Big Bend. She has noticed something new in her clients, generally people busted for smuggling drugs. They tell her they were forced into moving drugs, and that if they refused their families would be killed.

But that is not what strikes her.

It is their indifference when sentenced to federal prison. They tell her they would rather go to prison than be sent back to Mexico.

She believes them.

Something is happening across the river and it is death.

She was raised on the border. She has been a federal defense attorney for a long time and heard all kind of lies.

But almost against her will, she believes what she is being told, that there is something now loose across the river that is far more frightening than the prospect of spending years in a federal prison cell.

Eagle Pass came early and became the first US settlement on the new line created by theft in the Mexican War. The area just to the south was settled by Seminoles, some black, all refugees from American armies slaughtering them in Florida and then deporting them to Oklahoma. Mexico gave them shelter and land as a barrier against Indian raids. After the Civil War, they became US Army scouts in the wars against the Comanches. And then, when the tribes on the southern plains were crushed, the black Seminole scouts were cut loose and their participation was largely erased and only got revived with the civil rights movement in the 1960s.

But they were here, serving the US Army at the fort in Eagle Pass. Across the river is Piedras Negras, a town that recently has become murderous like large patches of Mexico.

Grackles feed on the lush grass in the baking heat. The commanding officers' quarters are now a children's library.

Across the river people disappear and then the silence closes over their abductions. From Eagle Pass, Mexico looks a peaceful green with a cathedral in the background.

Falcon Lake

Two simple ideas must be held in the mind at the same time: Mexicans are murdered wholesale in Mexico and violence is not spilling across the border.

Falcon Lake demonstrates these facts.

Last year, a House committee visited with a Zeta in the Zapata County jail. The guy was nineteen and had been busted moving four hundred pounds of marijuana across the lake. He started his career at fifteen being a lookout, and graduated to smuggling. In a two-year period, he'd run two to three hundred loads across the lake for five grand a trip. The lake has loads going day and night, something successful bass fishermen ignore. The retired smuggler also killed eighteen or nineteen people by his count, mainly members of the organization who failed to pay or who broke some rule. He said a cattle trough was the favorite kill site. He also noted that the best place to enter the US illegally was behind a grocery store in Laredo that is next to the McDonalds. He hoped to trade knowledge of a mass grave for his release and if successful, planned to join the US Army where he thinks his killing talents will be rewarded. All this is in the House report, a document that borders on hysteria as it scours the border looking for some of that violence spilling over the line.

I sit in a restaurant on the US side of the lake. The place

has been open seven months and seats at least 150 at rose-wood tables. The bar is horseshoe-shaped with a fine wall of liquors. I ask for red wine and the bartender wants to know if I like it hot or cold. No one can figure out how to remove the cork and finally they extract it without bothering to remove the foil cap. I sit in the place twice for say two hours. I never see another customer ask for food. Or drink. The staff sits around and drinks. There is a motel attached and no one seems to go there either. They are building a new wing onto the structure.

Drugs cross the lake in the day and the night and the proceeds from this toil must be washed and made fit for the American economy and the bankers that count the change.

The south wall of the restaurant is all glass and I watch the calm waters lap against the shore in a small cove.

PART II

Juárez

I am hearing voices.
   At first, I believed the voices.
   Then I thought I must be imagining them.
   Now I no longer wonder if they are real or imagined.
   It does not matter because of what I have learned from the voices.
   I am dirty, covered with mud.
   One of the voices told me this fact.
   I am an accomplice now.

There is a woman running, running and no matter how hard she runs, he catches up and the bullets slam into her head.
   I watch her run.
   Over and over again.

I begin with no end in mind. I avoid a career. I leave secure jobs. I travel, sleep in a truck, eat bad sandwiches, swallow black coffee in bleak diners. This goes on for years and then I realize I am forty and there will never be a normal life for me.
   That is how I find Juárez and I find it everywhere. I am not looking for violence or stories. I want shattered ground so that the light pours in and nothing can hide in the shadows.

I am drawn to people falling through space. I reach out to grasp their hands as we career into the void together.

This is the only way I can feel safe.

This is my home.

*   *   *

The other day I was walking past a table of books in a store and suddenly the letters on the covers fluttered and kept shifting and the words of the people speaking around me became babble as the various syllables in the words also fluttered and rearranged and I could for a brief instant understand nothing. I thought: this must be what a stroke feels like. Then it lifted and meaning returned.

With my time among the violent, there is a variation of this feeling.

The words, the sounds, the meanings all seem the same and then for brief instants seem to fly apart and lose all meaning or they hide other meanings that are foreign to my life. This is the learning that draws me, this is the ignorance I keep trying to escape.

But at most I can only glance at the world of violence. I cannot live it and I cannot imagine it. I am too humdrum.

There is the matter of ego also.

I don't think I could stand living in fear, either.

That is why I became an accomplice.

I have been asked why I pay attention to such people when there are fine things about life to record and explore.

I will never live long enough to understand why any human being would ask such a question.

I don't want to understand such a question.

I keep smelling the soil in spring, the raw aroma of life coming, and I think of seed catalogues and tomatoes in a row and the way radishes roar out of the ground, the power of beans tossing earth aside and reaching up for the sun.

Still, I hear the voices, see the woman run and then be gunned down.

*   *   *

We are drinking in the yard under the pecan tree.

The river is near.

For years, I have told him to get out while he can, for years I have told him the violence will become too great. He has always refused to leave because he will not abandon his country.

Now he tells me he has gotten his papers in order. Now he tells me he may have to leave.

I say I'll help.

Chekhov always argued that if a gun appears in the first act of a play it must be fired by the third act. I don't think so. In Mexico, the gun may never appear, can be fired at any moment and a body will fall to the floor with no explanation. Or a machete will suddenly lop off a head and yet no hand seems connected to the machete and no explanation will be offered for the decapitation. Dawn will find your body lying on a pile of rubble. You will be carried away to the morgue, then catalogued and eventually tossed into a hole in the ground.

Your life will have that narrative arc and in the third act you will be killed.

But no one will hear the gun go off.

And no one will know why you died.

And more and more often no one will know who you are.

Outside of these points, Chekhov was right about the nature of plays.

*   *   *

He walks to his office door in the early morning light.

A red truck pulls up beside him with a young guy and his woman.

The guy says, "You shouldn't be doing what you are doing. And we know where your daughter is."

This is not the first time.

You don't get used to it.

He continues on to court and files the papers.

But you don't get used to it.

*   *   *

At gray light squads of crows come up from the river to the scattered popcorn on the black asphalt by the barbershop. A three-hundred-pound man climbs from the small car, his white shirt billowing like a main sail. The ambulance screams down the six-lane road.

Five bodies are found downriver piled on some broken rubble. They look lonely sprawled out on the ground. Their clothing no longer looks stylish as the morning light washes across it. Little numbered cones frame the bodies where the officials track various bullets and casings. It will all go into a file and the file will go into a box and the box will go into a stack and then eventually all of this will wind up in the dump.

They are all quite young,

The neighbors say they heard the girl yell, "Don't kill me."

El Sicario

The afternoon light brushes the faded white table as his brown hands wave in the air. His solid body looms against the half-opened blinds. He has a mustache and goatee today, and his hair is short but still unruly. He wears a long-sleeved white T-shirt, slacks, boots. He is on the edge of leave-taking, he has been on this edge for months.

They are getting closer, he says.

They are getting younger, he says.

They will kill me, he says.

You don't understand, he says.

This is my life we are talking about, CHAR-LES, he says.

Always, my name is broken in half.

His voice rumbles, his voice hits odd boyish highs and breaks, his voice drops low and seeks a way to express inner secrets.

My eyes drift and I see a goldfinch out the window.

His voice pulls me back in.

He says when he goes out now he sees them, sees them at the corner store, sees them in church, sees them in cafes.

He must escape.

His time is almost up.

I am ordered to write it down.

I pull out a blue notebook and write with black ink.

He watches with solemn approval.
This is to be a testament.
Write.

*   *   *

My legs are sore from chiggers.

    But I keep wearing shorts because I must feel the light and the air.

    A wild turkey stands and stares.

    In the night, owls hooted along the creek and the hummingbirds slept off the gallon and a quarter of sugar water they swallowed yesterday. In the night, my mind went blank because I could no longer think about things beyond my reckoning.

    In the morning, the horses broke out and wandered down the lane. Then two vaqueros came and fixed the fence. In the morning, a vast whirring of hummingbirds descended on the feeders and with the light, yellow and blue-black butterflies clustered and sought sugar water. Back in New Orleans in a twenty-eight-hour span they managed four murdered and four more wounded.

    I hear the clack of beaks as two hummingbirds war in the early gray light.

    The squirrel falls off the feeder and looks surprised.

    The light on the ground is shifting from white to yellow as summer begins to sag. The nights have fallen down to sixty degrees.

*   *   *

I take no chances.

    I am the quiet man who watches birds. Or I am the man who claims to watch birds.

Things get in the way at times but there are some con-
stants.

I am a coward.

I am tired of the killing.

I am pointless.

I look but do not act.

I listen and write things down and my words change
nothing.

I stand in the sun and listen to the songs from the trees,
scan for a Cooper's Hawk, hear the white wings toll and think
I will never write one more word about murder or violence.

The phone rings.

And I say yes to the request.

I am a fraud who must remain true to my mission.

That is the way things go in the valley of dry bones.

Jericho

The first march in Selma, Alabama, busted heads on a Sunday and when the beatings looked out from television screens there was alarm in the land that such things happened. The second march got turned around by a federal court order but afterwards the Rev. James Reeb, a Unitarian Universalist out of Boston, was clubbed by angry white people and he died.

The people there, especially young black kids from Selma, started doing riffs on "The Battle of Jericho." Improvisations that went like this: "We got a rope that's a Berlin Wall, Berlin Wall . . . in Selma, Alabama. . . . We're gonna stand here 'til it fall. . . . Hate is the thing that built the wall. . . . Love is the thing that will make it fall. . . .

And eventually the people march to Montgomery, Alabama, and Martin Luther King stands on the steps of the state capitol building, and gives the speech that came to be called "How Long, Not Long."

But parts of the speech left his printed text and parts of that speech never made the published versions. One of those parts cast aside later by folks with calmer judgment recalls a city where the walls fell down, and Martin Luther King says to the multitude that when the men of Joshua walked around the walled city of Jericho, "the barriers for freedom came tumbling down." He then recalls an old spiritual from slavery times and he says it out loud:

Joshua fit the battle of Jericho
Joshua fit the battle of Jericho . . .
Go blow dem ram horns, Joshua cried
Cause de battle am in my hand.

And he said to the multitude that in order to have a society
at peace with itself, that can live with its conscience, it must
have patience. No matter how frustrating the hour, "it will
not take long."

And then night fell, and the world went dark, and Viola
Liuzzo, a white woman from Detroit with five children who
had come down alone to Selma, Montgomery, because she
got upset by those images of beatings on the television got in
her car filled with black people from the march to give them
a ride back to Selma and a car of whites pulled up beside her
out on the open road and put two bullets in her head and as
she passes from life to death maybe she still hears the words
said that afternoon, "How long?" Not long, because "no lie
can live forever."

After Viola Liuzzo lay dead some local people said she'd
really come down to have sex with black men. The FBI leaked
slurs about her. After Viola Liuzzo was dead it came out that
one of her killers was an FBI informant. He was given im-
munity for his testimony. His fellow Ku Klux Klan members
were acquitted of murder charges. And Viola Liuzzo became
the dead woman who was a bad mother and left her family
and then came whispers about what she was doing in Alabama with black men.

The Cranes

The sounds are hard to pin down. Aldo Leopold made a stab at catching the calls of sandhill cranes. The flock at a distance sounds, he thought, like "a tingling of little bells," then as it nears it is "the baying of sweet throated hounds," and finally, when it arrives, well, that was the moment Leopold's words began to fail him and he wrote they become a "pandemonium of trumpets, rattles, creaks and cries."

They begin early. A trilling sound starts inside the egg ten to thirty-nine hours before hatching and this sound is constant. The parents purr back at the eggs. The scientists think this behavior imprints and so a chick knows the sound of its parents before it ever breaks out into the light of day. Soon they have mastered five calls—a purring when happy or feeding with their parents, a peeping when they beg for food, a loud call when cold, hungry or lost, a high-frequency call when about to take off and an alarm call of broken notes when scared. More calls are added when they become adults, including a set of purring notes when they want to mate.

They are a nation and have their own tongue.

* * *

In New Orleans the talks are also over, the business groups, the artists. So are the lunches and long coffees. It hardly matters: what I say stands off to the side and the real world, the decent world, the only world that matters, has nothing to do with what I say and stares at it askance.

Each day I pass a park near the state capitol building. Illegal men huddle there in the cold and hope for some offer of work. When I mention them to others, they say, yes, yes, and then the conversation moves on and the men in the park become invisible once again.

In Ciudad Juárez, neighbors have blocked two thousand streets in an effort to shelter themselves from killers.

In Ciudad Juárez, a third of the houses have been abandoned.

In Ciudad Juárez, there are ten thousand new orphans, a hundred thousand abandoned dogs.

In Ciudad Juárez. . . .

No one questions what I say.

They seem to live it in their bad moments.

The sun helps but still it is not enough. I sit outside and read for hours with it burning my face. It is part of keeping the words away. For eight weeks I cannot construct a simple sentence. Thoughts stay just out of reach. I am able to respond. If someone says something, I can disagree.

But I cannot build anything with my mind.

At first I like this state. But then I realize I cannot escape it and I find myself in this cage of silence. At night, I wonder if my former self will ever return. During the day, I watch birds and this seems enough. But at night the fear returns, the sense of emptiness.

I become sensitive to sounds. If someone raises their voice, I want to run and hide or I want to kill them on the spot with my bare hands.

Slowly, this begins to change.

I remember trying to write a letter of recommendation, trying for days and then weeks. Finally, I manage the task.

The letter, like all such statements, is a lie. Still, I am struck that I could write it out and send it.

I feel that I am creeping back.

El Sicario

He tells me I am careless.

He tells me that my negligent ways show that I have never been tortured.

He can sense my innocence and he cannot forgive this.

I stare out the window at a goldfinch.

Write this down.

A man enters his house and is shot dead.

A man enters his house with his two daughters.

A man rides a bus, gets off, and enters his house with his two daughters.

A man enters his house and two other men meet him and take his two daughters to the patio and then shoot him dead.

A man enters his house and is shot dead and his wife is riding the bus and hears the gunfire but does not connect it to her man.

A man enters his house, meets two men who take his daughters to the patio, is shot dead, and his wife hears the gunfire and the man is thirty-three years old and a carpenter by trade.

The wife has a nervous crisis, the daughters are spared seeing their father's murder.

The man talking to me is correct, I have not been tortured and this is obvious.

No one has pulled out my fingernails, cut off my genitals, stuck an ice pick in the bones in my arm and then scraped. Gouged out an eye, cut off my tongue or arm or leg.

Delta

The land is seven feet above the sea and busy sinking. Signs on the road warn to watch for bears. The tiny sliver of ground is palmetto, cattails, ferns, moss-covered oaks, tupelo and cypress. The sea is very near and everyone knows the deep waters are coming.

The carillon stands by the edge and rises 106 feet. There are sixty-one bells running from eighteen pounds to 4,730. They are bronze.

Morgan City was first called Tiger Island. Now it is serene.

At the end of the week, a band plays near the sea wall, people drink beer and dance in the streets.

Southern Louisiana is going to go and someday the bells will sink into the mud.

But for now they say yes.

So do the dancers holding their beers beside the waters.

I carry a small blue notebook and I hope the color will lift me off the earth and fling me gibbering into the heavens.

I am in Livonia, Louisiana, and everything around me is green and everything above me is gray.

I follow back roads on Christmas Eve and men stack piles of wood for the coming bonfires as the dusk comes down. Fireworks rattle the night and then the rain comes.

———————

I am near the border and it is decades ago and I see a man in a white T-shirt, Camels folded in the sleeve, jeans, steel-toed workman's boots and he works the river, up and down on the boats from New Orleans to St. Louis. He is sitting on the couch while my father sits in the kitchen.

My old man told me a while back that about the time you figure life out, well, then you kick the bucket. Now he tells me little if nothing because they took him to the hospital, and chopped up his throat and tongue, and he's finished with words and left mainly to drooling and to scribbling short messages on Zig-Zag wheat straw rolling papers. A man with the whiskey comes into the kitchen and talks and asks questions and my father can do nothing but stare. The woman says leave him alone, he can't talk anymore, but the man with the whiskey pays them no mind—maybe because he's full of liquor, maybe because he's a little dumb—and my father stares at him mute.

All the furniture is used, the kitchen table, the mahogany one that seats ten in the dining room, the big hutch full of fine things that mean nothing now, silver, bone china, crystal, linens, embroidered things passed down from dead women who toiled by bad light in the evening in drafty farmhouses out on the plains, two carving knives embedded in wooden cases, strange mugs with faces that only emerge for Christmas alcohol, a room full of useless things that tally up the fine moments of a life, those days when the roast comes out and is sliced rare, the beans in a mushroom sauce, fresh bread, real butter, gravy in a sterling silver server, and I have never known the value of these things, these objects linking generations and I have not understood why they are coveted, polished, displayed and preserved. The old man is mute, the dining room is a warehouse of loot, the man with the pack of Camels and the bottle of whiskey keeps talking and asking questions and is oblivious of my father's inability to speak and I think maybe this is what history is, objects, words, scraps of things, a dash of whiskey and the claim of order and meaning.

He's got a bottle of Jack Daniels on the table and it is morning and he sips his whiskey. He's long dead as he sits before my eyes. I had hoped the blue notebook would stop these incidents. But now he is in the room and I am not sure why. Maybe he's back because I am standing on the soggy ground of southern Louisiana with the biggest thing around the lonely smokestacks of abandoned sugar refineries.

I can't keep the past in its casket.

And now I keep hearing the voices, the young guy with his whiskey, my father with his drool and mangled sounds. The old man will be dead in a month or two or three, no doubt puzzled why he ever helped finance a room full of stored china and tablecloths, especially since he seemed satisfied with a plate of corned beef hash served under a cloud of black pepper.

One of the women comes into the kitchen and barks, "Leave him alone, dammit, can't you see he can't talk," and walks out and the young guy swigs some more whiskey, the old man grunts and finally rolls a cigarette and resigns himself to a world empty of meaning.

I hear a rush of sound, music, a rhapsody, a word I can never explain but always know in my bones. The road curves along the river, the air is cancer, the feel is life, ditch, scum on water, I am a child and my aunt holds me as the smell off the bayou washes my face and I come out of the Mississippi River and she says nigger and the scent coming off her hateful skin that loves me is where I find my life, and decide my life, and the others around me deny my life.

I sit there, the air filled with smoke, the bottle of whiskey slowly emptying, the big meanings lost in the drone of humdrum things.

I hear my father's life story in the dead silence of his strangled voice.

El Sicario

First, brown some bacon, then, set it aside. Next brown a pan full of thighs. Set them aside. Toss in pearl onions, mushrooms, garlic and some flour, then bring back the chicken, add tomatoes, seasoning, and red wine. Simmer. Then remove all and reduce the sauce by a third. Add the bacon bits, the chicken, the vegetables. Serve over noodles made before dawn (two cups of flour, three eggs, rolled paper-thin).

The kitchen sags with scent.

I serve him a plate.

He prays over it.

He says it is very good.

He is planning his escape.

He sketches things out for me.

There is a window.

It opens, it closes.

Every seven days.

He wants me to know that he has put a lot of thought into his plan.

And now he puts me into his plan because there is no other way.

I give him more chicken, the wine sauce floating on the white plate. He takes some home to the wife, also.

He tells me I just want to be famous.

But that he could be killed.

CHAR-LES, this is my life we are talking about.
He tells me never to cross the border.
He tells me I don't know what torture feels like.

New Orleans

Imagine there is no mystery nor issue nor solution. That nothing is shocking, that all can be understood and that the real barrier between us and the seas rising and the bodies falling is acceptance. Of what is out there and what is going on inside us. That we know why people kill often in New Orleans, that we know why people kill often in Ciudad Juárez, that we know why the seas rise, that we know why the rains fail to come as they once did.

That we know.

That when we say we are shocked, we are liars.

That when we say a big wind raked New Orleans and revealed districts of poverty unknown to us, we are liars.

That when we hear Juárez is a very violent city, perhaps the most violent city on the surface of the earth and we knew nothing of this matter, we are liars.

That we know what is happening at sea, in the bayous, on the deserts, down the city lanes after darkness falls.

That we know of the poor, of the powerful and of our own greed and hungers.

I listen to the birds.

And they are not ignorant.

El Sicario

We ride around at night. He drives. He goes over the mountain, back down to the river, cuts in and out of neighborhoods. His eye is always on the rearview mirror and he keeps talking.

He cannot relax. He feels everything closing in on him. He has some kind of link to something, a warning system. Now he is getting warnings.

He tells of a cop on this side who works with the organization.

He tells of warehouses on this side.

How can they not know, he asks?

He must get out.

I make a call to an agency. To DEA. To CIA.

No one will deal with him.

I explain my product.

Has he killed?

We can't deal with people who have killed.

He keeps trying to explain: this is his life at stake. His family is at risk. Something must be done.

But we have reached some other country in our driving, a place where nothing will be done and nothing will be admitted. It is a matter of time. Then they find him and kill him and well, maybe the family also.

I am instructed by my lack of power.

Sometimes when he drives and talks and I stare out at the shops and cars and people I feel as if I am sealed in an aquarium, living under water, and no matter how loud I scream no one out there will hear, no one out there will listen.

I can understand their indifference.

It is a way of life.

Seventy, he says, seventy AKs he'd keep in the house, ten of them gold-plated for capos to carry at fiestas, and guns come down from the US, big truckloads of stuff and they hand them out to punks for hits and then the guns are returned.

I make a note.

But I have no idea why I make a note. There is no place to publish such a detail. I am not even certain I care about such details.

Once I was hungry for any glimpse inside this secret world. I would drive long distances; sit alone in a bleak motel room waiting for a call. I would spend money I did not have for a scrap of information. Sometimes a week would result in a single fact. I was ravenous.

I am no longer hungry.

Still, he must escape.

He sits there in the light by the white table but he is not looking at me, he is in that space where a person goes to speak and not be questioned, to intone and not be interrupted. The guns, yes, the guns are smuggled across in loads of clothing, he knows this, and the Mexican army knows this and does nothing and the FBI knows this and does nothing.

He falls into silence.

He is bitter over the fact that no one does anything.

This time.

Sometimes, he celebrates that fact, revels in this world of secret agreements and the stench of corruption, the world he knows and the one average people pretend does not exist.

Then he snaps out of this state, this stupor and says, "CHAR-LES, CHAR-LES, you are my accomplice and I thought long and hard before I spoke to you. I asked God, why should I trust him?

"I needed to make someone else part of this so that I could be at peace.

"I talked to God about this."

He seems to be floating now, almost weightless. He stares out and yet his eyes focus on nothing.

"You commit the same sin—the person who holds the cow is the same as the person who milks the cow.

"Now you are equally guilty.

"It is the only way I could feel comfortable."

The sun is setting, darkness comes down outside and now a fluorescent light bathes his face as he explains.

"I asked God, should I trust him?

"The first time, that was a test. I asked a friend if you were in the DEA. My friend said he did not know. So I took a chance.

"After the first interview, I had to be sure you were not setting a trap. So I found out where you lived so that if anything happened I could go after you.

"I prayed to God.

"Then I asked someone at my church. They said the idea was crazy and that they would not be part of my death.

"I prayed some more. I told myself if my friend called again, that would be a test and if he called then I would say yes.

"He called and so I said yes.

* * *

The hand of the LORD was upon me, and carried me out in the spirit of the LORD, and set me down in the midst of the valley which was full of bones, and caused me to pass by them round about: and, behold, there were very many in the open valley; and, lo, they were very dry. And he said unto me, Son of man, can these bones live? And I answered, O Lord GOD, thou knowest. Again he said unto me, Prophesy upon these bones, and say unto them, O ye dry bones, hear the word of the LORD. Thus saith the lord GOD unto these bones; Behold, I will cause breath to enter into you, and ye shall live: And I will lay sinews upon you, and will bring up flesh upon you, and cover you with skin, and put breath in you, and ye shall live; and ye shall know that I am the LORD. So I prophesied as I was commanded: and as I prophesied, there was a noise, and behold a shaking, and the bones came together, bone to his bone. And when I beheld, lo, the sinews and the flesh came up upon them, and the skin covered them above: but there was no breath in them. (Ezek. 37:1–8)

* * *

I never saw this coming. I anticipated the tests. I suspected the prayers. I was certain that my life was forfeited if I lied and betrayed him. All of that.

But this confession, this soliloquy as afternoon fades into night, this I never saw coming. Something is ending, this is a leave-taking. I can understand that. But I never expected such a courtesy.

I knew things had slowly changed, that we had grown closer, but I also knew some things can never change, that real trust is impossible when one person can send the other person to his death. I knew that if I were him, I would never really trust me.

I was not after trust but understanding. In the beginning, I just wanted to learn. I expected nothing beyond that possibility.

He says, "Another test was when I let you learn my real

name in that Chihuahuan newspaper. I thought if you reveal that, we will both go down together."

I look up from my blue notebook. I remember that moment and two things strike me and show my limits. It never occurred to me to reveal that name. And I was never sure it was his real name. For me the test was of a different order: he'd revealed a name to see if I would expose the name but I assumed if he'd let me learn that name it was a fake name.

I have been living in a hall of mirrors and I have taken this experience as normal.

He says, "You became complicit because you knew my real name. Now you are tied to me by your knowledge. You are covered with mud."

Everything he says I know, even the things he has not said before and that I have not thought before.

What we have done together has not been simply telling a story and I have known that. Nor have we ever admitted why we were doing it. He has been an informant. I have been a writer. This has been a convenient lie.

And now, before he vanishes forever, he insists the lies cease.

I lean back in my chair. I have now spent almost two years scratching words on pieces of paper as he speaks. Some of this has never been published and maybe it never will be published. I have spent considerable sums on journeys. I have earned no profit.

His wife asks him about me. She wants to know, "Why does he do this?"

She is puzzled because it is obvious there is no money for me in this thing.

"All of this stuff," he begins, "about the people buried . . ." and his voice trails off and I remember it all and I look up because I have carried unknown graveyards around in my mind for months.

I would sit and stare at photographs and know thirty people are secretly buried in that hole, a half dozen or more rot under that swimming pool. I would think of going to these places but I would know that if I did, it could catch someone's notice and trigger trouble. I thought of sending others but then I thought this could get them into real trouble and I could not even tell them why I wanted them to visit such places.

Nor could I talk to many people about it. And then, something happened, and he said I must keep my silence on these things he had taught me. He had noticed the people seeking to kill him were getting closer, getting younger. So he insisted on caution, and I buried my knowledge of the dead people and, just like their corpses, this knowledge ceased to really exist.

And his voice returns and he says, "I couldn't tell this to a minister or priest because they wouldn't know what to do with it. But you are a crazy writer and you will know when to do something with it."

Ah, he is back to lecturing me. It is essential that I remain the student and he the teacher. After all, I am free and he is doomed. The people hunting him are just like him and he seldom failed in his hunts and he can hardly expect any less of them.

So, he lectures and this gives him comfort.

He says, "Most people are not prepared for the truth. You are open. I knew you would ask certain questions and I prepared for you and I never said more than I planned to say."

I nod.

And I know he lied to me for months and months and then suddenly told me something he'd insisted he knew nothing about.

And I know I asked him about something and he told me he would never reveal that to me and then one day sat down and could not stop talking about it.

And I know the first time I met him he said nothing could leave the room and I instantly started making notes and he did nothing.

And I know that the second time I met him, he said he would no longer speak and we went into a room and he spoke for hours.

Some kind of line was crossed when we made the film because neither one of us could simply justify it. For him, it was a lethal decision. And for both of us it took us into a territory, a hard ground where facts became ground glass ripping apart our bare feet.

I remember him sobbing.

I'm sure he does also.

But we never speak of those moments.

Yet some kind of line was crossed.

And we never came back.

* * *

Then said he unto me, Prophesy unto the wind, prophesy, son of man, and say to the wind, Thus saith the Lord GOD; Come from the four winds, O breath, and breathe upon these slain, that they may live. So I prophesied as he commanded me, and the breath came into them, and they lived, and stood up upon their feet, an exceeding great army. (Ezek. 37: 9–10)

* * *

He is speaking again.

He will not stop.

"A friend told me that people will say anything for money. But I said, no one could pay the price of what I tell them. If told the story of my conversion, no one would care about my life. Christians, like me, we really like stories about our lives as sinners before we were saved. But I am not trying to reach Christians, but sinners."

This is a point he can never let go of. He has put his life at risk, he has trusted me against his better instincts, he has put his family at risk and all of this has to be in order to reach sinners or it cannot be justified.

"The people in the church know God can save a killer but I wanted the world to know that.

"The message is very short.

"In the article you wrote, a few pages.

"In the film, eighty minutes.

"God only needs a few minutes to touch people."

And night is heavy now, there is nothing but darkness, he keeps sitting there by the white table. His hands keep waving, he is in some deep part of himself now and I am barely a presence, I am simply this person with a notebook who writes down his words. I asked a single question and he spoke for two days and later I found this tiny note with half a dozen words and I realized he had come with his own movie in his head and this movie was what life had taught him and my questions were of no importance.

And he was right.

"About the movie, at first I was worried about it, worried it might be shown in Mexico. Now I don't care. It has been shown in France, Germany and Italy and I sit up at night reading comments and many people think I am a monster and my wife asks, 'Why do you read these things about you?' I say I have to, I cannot stop and they say really terrible things about me and I think God will protect my family. I think I will be able to leave here."

I sit up. I realize he has entered another country, a place that is fatal for him. He has entered the land of hope.

* * *

Then he said unto me, Son of man, these bones are the whole house of Israel: behold, they say, Our bones are dried, and our hope is lost: we are cut off for our parts. Therefore prophesy and say unto them, Thus saieth the lord GOD; Behold, O my people, I will open your graves, and cause you to come up out of your graves, and bring you into the land of Israel. And ye shall know that I am the LORD, when I have opened your graves, O my people, and brought you up out of your graves, and shall put my spirit in you, and ye shall live, and I shall place you in your own land: then shall you know that I the LORD have spoken it, and performed it, saith the LORD. (Ezek. 37: 11–14)

*   *   *

It is time to turn out the light.

He is scrambling now to make sense of things. He says I am an atheist. He says I worship the sun.

He says he has a plan and he draws this plan on a sheet of paper and his plan looks very much like all the other such plans I have seen. He will avoid the traps, go around the agents, and take his family to safety. He will get a job and he will work hard and he will pray and he will each day try to pay in some fashion for his many sins and murders and tortures.

He will make up for his life if he is allowed to live.

I go over maps with him.

I say, be careful, they hide here.

I say, if you get to this point, they cease to hunt you.

He says I will never hear from him again.

I nod.

I knew this time would come, I knew this time must come.

The window opens every seven days. That is how government checkpoints work—a person must slip through based on the schedule of an agent who works for the government. There is always a fee. There are always complications. There is always a ruse, a set of things and attitudes and dress and mannerisms that will put the authorities at ease.

He is talking now, making drawings.

The map spreads on the table.

He lists expenses.

Tells of safe houses, way stations and the like. It was surely this way with people whispering in the slave cabins before they climbed aboard that idea called the underground railroad. He thinks they should travel as a unit, then again maybe it is better if they split up. He has a list of connections, people and places that will take him in while he is still in flight.

I half listen. I don't want to know too much detail. I don't want to accidentally give him away.

He is meticulous in drawing out his plans. He has spent many hours going over this and he focuses in the same way, I am sure, he once focused on a murder contract.

"CHAR-LES, this is my life we are talking about."

That is what he would say when we drove around at night and I sketched out possible ways for him to sell his knowledge to US agencies. But they were not interested.

I am struck by certain things people tell me. One is that I should never have had anything to do with this person and that his story should never be told. The other is that he is evil. The other is that I face a moral obligation, and should turn him in to some authority.

I go back to considering his plan. I am sure it can work. I have no doubt about finding and paying corrupt agents. Others have, surely he can.

CHAR-LES.

I am more with him than with my friends who tell me he is evil. I am more with him than I am with my government that has set up roadblocks to control the flow of human beings not on the approved list.

And I am more with him than the people who denounce

him as a monster. Not because I overlook his acts but because I live now in a world where governments pay for his acts.

He tells me my problem is that I have not been tortured.

Others tell me my problem is that I insist he is normal.

We cannot turn away from each other.

We have faced the great death and not lied about it to each other and not known what to do and not claimed we knew more than others but simply that we denied less.

We have almost nothing to say.

He waits for God to make a move.

I wait for others to notice God has left the building.

The Cranes

At age two, maybe three, cranes come into their own, look for mates and open up their hearts in a way few humans would risk. They begin the unison call. It is a duet between male and female cranes, and can last a few seconds to a minute. Over time a mated pair's unison call gets more and more elaborate and since cranes live decades, and mate for life, this joint music is the work of a lifetime.

They are standing side by side, the male with his beak pointing straight up to the heavens, the female with her head at a forty-five-degree angle, his call answered by two or three shorter calls from her, musically an antiphonal duet. It claims ground, it frightens off predators, but mainly it says two birds are really one and is repeated during the day like a common prayer.

The Delta

We are in the valley of dry bones. In Louisiana I get up in front of the congregation and read the passages from Ezekiel to them and it feels like a feathery hand passing over their faces in the glow of the southern sun by the green-laced water of the bayous. I think of étouffée and bread pudding drenched with rum and of thin fillets of catfish and gumbo and hot sauces splashed like holy water. A woman comes up and says her name is Larry. A woman comes up and says her name is Jon. I read Ezekiel and we all wander in the valley of dry bones and lick remoulade off our fingers and outside the old smokestacks of the vanished sugar refineries stand as sentinels over an erased past, the clang of slave chains gone, the row of shacks in the quarters tumbled down and now rotted, the river kept behind levees, the ground sinking, the sea rising and everywhere little churches and old graveyards and they wait for the hurricane that will smash it all.

Everything that matters stands firmly on a floor of red beans and rice or it does not stand at all.

There was this moment after I read from Ezekiel in the little Baptist church by the bayou when I stepped outside and I wrote in my blue notebook: When you bring me some red meat, we can talk about butchering.

Stories, lives, tales, all fall down, all flee through the checkpoints.

Guns in the case, a three-point buck on the wall that weighed two eighteen and across the levee is the Atchafalaya River and on the kitchen counter fresh corn bread, sweet potatoes, dirty rice, turkey, pecan pie and in the other room a collection of Aunt Jemima statues and one son says, "If you bring one more colored person into this home, we're going to throw them all away," and there is a hutch, the one Bubba made and he says, "The wood came from an abandoned mill, one owned by an old widow lady, and the cypress still has the mill marks and I did nothing but put some wax on it, see the ridges left by the saw? And the glass is that Depression glass with waves in it," and he rubs his hand on the wood. He hunts "most every day, see that big gun? That was my grandfather's shotgun.

"I was over in my uncle's shop and he said, see that gun? And I said yes, and he said that was your granddad's and I killed my first deer with it.

"My Dad once ran over my sister, he had a '49 one-ton and he was backing it up and couldn't see her and he run over her and he thought he'd killed her and I saw it happen, I was over by the ditch and she didn't have one broken bone.

"The nine-year-old boy? He's fine. Fell out of the pickup when we were putting out deer corn. Busted his pelvis is all. Out at the hunt club."

Bubba is on a roll. The swamp is near, the deer thick in there, and this is a far distance from the man fleeing with his family, the man who used me to tell his story of his killings. This is Louisiana and another country and Bubba says, "Larry, he was thirty-five, taught ninth grade at the school and then he got his pilot's license and they found his plane burned up. Just as well probably. His family didn't grieve none and he just disappeared because he'd shot his ex-wife.

Been flying to Colombia, they land right over there on the river, when I lived over there I'd see them landing, pontoon planes, doors would open and then they'd barely be on the water and they'd be gone again, sometimes they'd wave at me and there were some Mexicans down there and where do the planes come from? I don't know.

"I've never smoked, done drugs or drunk anything. Well, once at hunt camp I got up and had a big glass of orange juice and that was the last thing I remember and I never drank anything again where I wasn't sure what was in it."

They think a football field of ground is lost to the sea here every thirty-eight minutes. The kids sit on the floor shooting darts from their blowgun into a pillow off the couch. It's Christmas, sky gray, spats of rain and deer moving through the swamps in the gray light, about to slap on a video about how to hunt them and find one with a big rack and the planes are still coming up the river, landing on pontoons briefly, off-loading onto small boats and then taking off and there's Mexicans down by the river you know and the man sits at the white table and waves his brown hands and says, CHAR-LES, this is my life and he says the window at the checkpoint only opens once every seven days and even then you have to know who to ask and there is the question of what looks normal, the family all in one car? Or, in two cars?

This is the valley of the dry bones.

There are men coming to kill, and they are getting younger.

There are stories to be told.

Planes land on the river, unload and leave.

No plots.

No explanations.

Every seven days the window opens and escape is possible. I do two things when I sense he is gone, when I feel confident his lies and tricks and evasions have come to an end and he is over some kind of horizon, the one where he promised I would never find him again and never hear from him again.

I get two plants, French tarragon and creeping rosemary.

It has been a hard winter and there was bitter cold.

Things must begin again.

Even though they have never ended.

I can still hear him praying over the food I would give him.

He is not happy I cooked with wine. He no longer has vices.

Just nightmares.

Jericho

Moses tells the people they have a choice. He is old now, a hundred and twenty years and finds moving hard on his body. He will never cross that Jordan River into Canaan. Joshua will. But Moses leaves this last warning to the people and tells them they can choose life or death. He says, "I call heaven and earth to record this day against you, that I have set before you life and death, blessing and cursing: therefore choose life, that both thou and thy seed may live."

I feel a breeze on my neck, hear the hawk high above, a killer with white feathers when seen from below as it rides thermals seeking to have a life by delivering death.

The people of Israel pause, the river is before them, if they cross they earn life, if they cross Jericho falls and everyone inside the city. It is in the book, it must be done. God's will.

The hawk stoops. I watch the dive.

On April 7, 1965, Lyndon Baines Johnson reads these same Bible lines from Deuteronomy in a speech as he sketches out his offer to North Vietnam—development or the armed might of the United States of America. Privately, he told confidants he would never accept his offer if he were them, because they were winning.

On May 23, Martin Luther King stands in Atlanta and tells his flock at Ebenezer that he has been to the mountaintop, that he has seen the promised land. He is thirty-six years old. He has slightly less than three years to live.

El Sicario

The movie plays on the screen and I rewind the scene over and over. He leans over my shoulder and stares. A woman stands in front of the state capitol in Chihuahua. It is night and the film is black and white and the product of a security camera.

The woman is protesting the murder of her daughter. Her killer confessed to the murder, there was a trial before three judges and the judges set him free.

Now she stands and protests. A man comes up with a gun, she runs, he chases her. And puts bullets inside her skull. Cars drive by. No one comes to her aid.

The man leans over my shoulder.

He stabs his finger and says "There, that car pulling over picks up the killer. But this car, the one behind, blocks traffic so that they can flee. This is well done, professional."

I stare at the screen. The first car pauses, the man leaps in, then the car turns the corner and goes out of sight. The second car pauses, the woman lies on the ground, her head full of lead.

No matter how often I play it, she races away, is caught, murdered and then her killer escapes.

The man leans over my shoulder.

The message is: Will the man appear on television for an interview?

The answer is: Are you crazy?

He is gone now.

He is moving down a highway.

He has escaped.

That is what he thinks.

That is what we all want.

I can still hear him saying there, there, that car is part of the unit, that car is blocking, there, everyone slows, no one is going to interfere, no one.

He will get away.

He has it all planned.

He will be careful.

In the film, the woman keeps running and the man keeps chasing her.

In the film, she does not make it.

CHAR-LES, this is my life we are talking about.

PART III

The Line

His people have farmed on the Rio Grande since the eighteenth century.

"They've got this old Spanish land grant," he says, "but with the Mexican war that all got stolen by the Americans. That's okay, my people stole it from the Indians."

Now he wears a uniform, Border Patrol. He's been at it many years. He is fit.

At first, he stops by to have coffee and pick my brain.

I am alone and at night trucks pass on the dirt road with lights off and the flatbeds loaded. They stash the kilos across the creek in a small clearing just off the road, or here and there along the creek. Sometimes I run into the mules, dressed head to toe in black, who have finished toting their loads twenty miles or so, neatly stacked them, and left them in the care of a man with a gun. About once a summer, a load is discovered by the authorities and then makes a small splash in the newspapers. The rest of the year, things hum along without such noise.

He picks my brain. Have I seen anything? Noticed anything?

It is a professional habit, this harvesting of little details that might lead to a bust and then a case.

I always tell him the same thing.

I watch birds.

He nods.

And sips his coffee.

He still believes in the border.

There are problems, he knows that, he is not a fool.

I ask one day over coffee just how many people he trusts that he works with.

He falls silent.

Then says softly, "No one."

Picus, Number 7

A different man is talking to me. He is very excited by the story he is telling. He speaks for hours and hours about a killing and what led up to it. The things announced by federal agencies in the newspapers, or spread as rumors on the Internet, he despises.

And he can be honest, he explains, because this killing in the newspapers is not that important. The killer and the killed are not really big men. They can be talked about with some safety.

Yes, he will tell me, he says, what really happened.

He insists on it.

I remember talking on the phone to an editor in New York.

He says, yes, that one sounds good, the one about killing a drug guy. Yes.

I can almost hear his lips smacking.

I need the money, that is part of it. And I think of the man who keeps talking to me, how he wants the story put down on paper. So I agree.

But I know it will be nothing but grief. The characters will not be grand enough, they never are. The people in the drug industry have their moments but mainly they scramble from one deal to the next and watch over their shoulder for the death they know reaches out to choke their life away.

One other fact will cause me grief: they are brown and that means they are outside the interests of mainstream publications. Still, it is possible in this case because, after all, they are criminals and that helps make them acceptable.

But still there is the problem of not being grand.

They never are. They are the poor carving new lives out of the hungers and lies of governments.

The man talking, he does not think of such matters. He lives in a world and it is his entire world and now he wishes to speak. He eyes gleam. He is busy drawing charts, recording the genealogy of his tribe and people.

The man's story begins simply. He is a predator offering a kill as a present, the cat leaving the rat on the doorstop.

The man recounting the story sees nothing strange in the tale, and nothing very significant. He laughs as he speaks, says the story should be easy to check out, just look for a woman with fingers cut off of one hand.

I never ask him why he tells me the story. He wants it known, I realize, and his reasons are his own. He is using me.

He starts by talking about how the trouble began for Picus, which means pointy. It is a September day, he explains, when Number 12 is murdered and Number 7 proves not up to the job.

I write down the numbers.

The speaker pauses now, he is back in his world and I am someone to entertain. He knows I would never last a minute in the life. I am not tough enough. I have not suffered enough. There is a veil over his world and though he will lift one corner and let me glimpse within, he makes it clear that I do not belong there and will never fully understand what he is telling me.

There is the matter of the life, *la vida loca*, and it is terrible and it is evil and yet it is life at full volume with no boundaries. But you can have women, snap, just like that, and others fear you and you have money and can eat and drink and the rules that control others do not exist for you and the terror and edge that you taste cannot even be imagined by others.

He looks over at me to make sure that I am making notes. I am his secretary and I must write down his words. He has crossed all the lines and he wants a record made of lives and deaths he has known. He sighs. He has his own pad of paper also and he sets out to sketch with names and arrows, the power relationships of a world beneath common notice, a world that runs the public world but does it from the shadows.

For him borders do not mean much. You cross from one nation to another, you cross from decency to evil, you wear a police uniform or you kill a cop, you are past the lives of others as you scream toward something even you cannot imagine—your own death. And it all feels so fine.

Your habits matter. Number 12 has a habit of showing up at discos with twenty or thirty people and a harem of good-looking women. He's a flashy guy—he and his men wear $4,000 boots. He drinks too much, and gets loud. If he feels like it, he will have a guy beaten for just looking at him. He headed the police anti-kidnapping squad, then joined organized crime and spawned a few small businesses on the side.

This is the feel of the story, the excitement of the life, the swagger and then comes judgment day and there is nothing to be done because judgment is final and there is no place for appeal.

Number 12's noisy behavior bothers Don Vicente Carrillo, who has run the Juárez drug organization since his brother died in 1997. Some incidents are bad for business and ruffle the feathers of people in government who, after all, are partners in the operation. At least, that is the way things were viewed in normal times before the explosion of killings that burned all the rule books. Don Vicente believes in a rational standard of death, where Ciudad Juárez has two hundred to two hundred and fifty murders a year and his organization accounts for maybe half of them. Number 12 is told to quiet down. For two years, he does. But, then Number 12 regresses, which upsets Don Vicente.

Four or five years earlier, Number 12 was supervising marijuana growers in the Sierra Madre for the Juárez organization. The growers thought he had cheated them and so he took a barrage of rounds. Before that moment, he was a good kidnapper and killer. But as he lay there on the edge of death, he vowed to the Virgin that if his life were spared, he would not kill again. He lived, and continued his work—the kidnappings and supervised murders—but he personally did not kill again. So when the men—federal and state police—arrive one morning as Number 12 is taking his infant daughter somewhere, he is constrained by this vow. He wears a 9mm in his waistband, but he is defenseless.

The men are kind. They move the baby to another car seat. Then they execute Number 12 in front of his house with sixty or seventy rounds, or forty rounds or thirty-three rounds—accounts vary—from AK-47s. When the killing is finished, a neighbor comes over and discovers the baby is fine except for the blood-soaked clothes and the fragments of glass. A servant of Number 12 finally answers the knocks on the door and takes the child.

There is this man and he has been kidnapped. They beat him with pistol butts and when he tries to escape they beat him with boards. He is moved from house to house in the car trunk. He can understand that. But when they take him out hands tied and he sees children playing on the street no one does anything, no one acts as if he exists. This he does not understand.

Once his blindfold slips and he sees the walls of the room where he is kept prisoner. The walls are covered with blood. At first he would lie on the floor blindfolded. The house they had taken him to was under construction. They would fire rounds by his head and say they were going to kill him.

They had him make phone calls.

And then it was back to a room, or back to the car trunk and another short trip. This went on for days. He could hear voices once and learned four federal police were being held in the same house.

He wished for death. No one ever seems to come back from these things and so he wished for it to be over and for the pain to end.

He had a boy, deeply autistic and in his life he would hold that boy and the boy would nuzzle him and become calm. Otherwise he would shriek. The boy makes him want to live. The beatings make him want to die. He gets water after the first day. Then there is the time he is given a ham sandwich. He hears men talking about which prisoner they will kill first.

He thinks it would be better to be shot down like a dog on the street than have the torture continue. Then, he thinks of his boy and then he cannot think anymore at all.

Finally, they let him go, toss him out on the street at five or six a.m. He runs and comes upon a car of federal policemen. They say, "We have been looking for you" and put him in a helicopter and fly him to the capital. Generals parade him on television as a proof of their victory in their war against crime. Then he is let out on the street with no protection. He calls his sister and she says strange gunmen with no uniforms are watching his home.

He flees with his family.

He cannot explain why he is alive.

He says, "I don't know, I don't know, I don't know."

The wounds on his head heal but leave scars.

He is a footprint left in the dirt by men like the one telling me the story.

Things have to work. Despite the nights on the town, the jewelry and women and guns, this is a business with bills, earnings, obligations, deliveries. The man telling the story knows this. He is all business and highly critical of personal errors. And yet he has spent much of his life in a business where there are constant mishaps. The murder of No. 12 eventually opens the way to No. 7, but in the disorder following the execution things drift and he thinks that is when Picus begins to stray and things go wrong.

I write as this splatter of men identified by numbers flows from his lips. I cannot quite follow things but that is the nature of such tales from the life, they are all details about unknown people and events seldom made public. So he talks and I make notes and for me it is like capturing the unraveling of a ball of tangled yarn.

Number 7 is promoted to take over the work—his uncle is a very connected guy. He proves to be a poor manager, which wouldn't matter except for the fact that, five years after Number 12 is murdered, his former colleague Picus shows up in US headlines:

POLICE INVESTIGATE CITY'S LATEST HOMICIDE
El Paso—A man was shot to death Friday night in far-east El Paso. The victim, a 30-year-old Hispanic male, was seriously wounded around 10 p.m.

Picus's real name is Jose Daniel Gonzalez Galeano. He lives in a $366,000, 3,300-square-foot house behind the residence of the chief of police in El Paso and is a businessman whose company, El Nuevo Rey, had reported annual sales of $84,000. His other businesses, all listing his home address, are Gonzalez Auto Parts, Letters and Colors Day Care, and Transportes Gonzalez.

He is also a high-level member of the Juárez organization. There are eight bullet holes.

When Gonzalez turns up dead, there is a flurry of speculation by security experts in the press that the violence plaguing Mexico has finally crossed over into the United States. The persistent fear of Americans, that it will come north, this thing ill-defined, never proven, always alluded to, something basic to Mexico that will cross the border. The experts also say that this killing on US soil of a significant member of the Juárez cartel is unprecedented.

What the experts like to call a cartel is actually a loose organization of drug merchants and employees and is in constant flux. As a joint effort to restrain competition, the organization has limited success since drugs keep getting cheaper and newcomers keep launching drug businesses. There are efforts at times to solve this problem by murdering interlopers. Death is part of maintaining order in the drug marketplace. No tale in this business can be sketched without people suddenly appearing and then disappearing as they kill and get killed.

I remember on the edge of the Sierra Madre being run off a dirt road by a red car that aimed right at me. I was heading to a drug village. The trees were in full flower that day and the hills shouted color and joy.

I turned around.

The drug industry creates a constant fog of war. People kill, kidnap, torture, move tons of drugs or millions of dollars and know little beyond the task at hand. They know the person who gives them orders but not that person's boss. They know there is a boss of the organization but will live and die without ever seeing that person. Sometimes they do not even know which organization they work for. US agencies create charts of the drug industry to convince themselves that all is orderly and logical and because of this tendency US agencies are always out of date. The drug industry itself is constant improvisation, endless shifting of workers, and a very high rate of attrition.

It is also one of the few things in Mexico that recognizes merit. In a nation where an Indian can seldom get a job beyond field work or pushing a broom, the drug industry salutes good managers of any background.

Almost anything can be said about the drug world because almost nothing is known but fragments. This tale is one such fragment. The man sits in front of me and talks. I can feel his presence. But he can never have a name or a face because that means death in this world. I think these slivers, these fragments, are the actual drug world. The thing discussed by the US agencies under the banner of the War on Drugs is a fantasy, one that consumes tens of billions of dollars in the financing of narcotics officers but still, it is a place imagined rather than real. It is a creation of US agencies and the agencies are also creations of this fantasy about life.

The life in the world is short and fueled by drugs, alcohol and fear. There is no long-term plan for most of the workers because they die before the long term.

The man telling me the tale, he works for years and leaves with nothing but the clothes he is wearing. But he leaves and at least stays alive for a while.

Nothing fits the official stories of violence spilling across the border, of walls needed to protect national security, of Mexicans being terrorists. Nothing in this story is about much of anything except business. Profit and loss.

This is an American story.

––––––

Picus is a self-made man who rises and then falls. In life and in death, he is a cipher used by politicians and agencies to describe whatever kind of world their budgets require.

He can be anything except what he was: a guy on the make who didn't quite make it.

The sun feels pale. The heat is gone. He leans down and stares toward the screen and follows the roll of the land. He looks fondly at the satellite image glowing in the room. This place, you must never go to this place, he says. Planes would come in all the time, loaded, and land here. It is one of the warehousing places.

The light of the screen plays across his face.

He keeps talking about the flights, how they come loaded out of the Sierra Madre like clockwork and how nothing happens, no one interferes.

The house in the desert has a red roof and backs up against a hill where it meets a big underground warehouse that stores tons of cocaine. A stream flows through the valley and is lined with irrigated fields. Ejidos, the collective communities founded after the Mexican Revolution, dot the landscape. The towns in the region are small, poor and dusty and named after Mexican heroes. This is a backwater.

I am sitting in a room being shown satellite images of the house with the red roof, where the men arrive in private planes for parties. They come in convoys of semis to offload shipments. They fly in on business. The ranch belongs to Don Vicente Carrillo, one of many such properties he owns, and the satellite pictures reveal nothing of the real function of the place.

Fiestas mean drugs, fine liquor and lots of women. There is also music, usually Norteño. The region is covered with a giant cobweb and the strands of this web connect airfields, warehouses, ranches, fine homes, death houses, safe houses —a separate society that mirrors the official society and sometimes runs the official society.

Cottonwoods line the stream by the isolated ranch, a green ribbon in the desert. Orchards flank the house and a big ditch brings water for the crops. Don Vicente loves farming and ranching. Before the death of his brother, Amado, he seemed more interested in using drug money to buy farms and ranches than he did in the drug industry itself. He also is very devout, a good Catholic.

But he makes sure his workers have parties.

The men are bringing women, lots of women, for a fiesta. They stay in a good hotel. One of the men flashes a gun at the desk clerk when checking in to ensure the staff knows who they are dealing with. He is drunk and takes forty cans of beer and rifles the till for 7,000 pesos. He has federal police identification. He does some cocaine in front of the staff. But he is all business—he is here to hire prostitutes for a party.

The next day the local police come when the hotel complains. There is the making of an incident and then it all goes away, even the small newspaper report. This is the feel of power and the man talking wants me to understand that he once belonged to this world, that he once could make incidents go away. Disappear people also.

There is this web spun over the nation, and Don Vicente, as head of the Juárez cartel, is one of the men who spins the web. And Picus becomes a tiny part of the web. That is, in the beginning.

Later, he grows and skitters across the web with ease.

Jose Daniel Gonzalez Galeano gets his nickname of Picus because of prominent front teeth and a hooked nose. He enters the drug life because of cheese. His family in Villa Ahumada, a town about ninety miles south of Juárez, manufactures dairy products and Picus has a border-crossing card so that he can haul cheese to El Paso. He starts small: a nobody from a nothing town running cheese and some dope into El Paso for the organization.

He is a calm man, and intelligent. He hardly talks, in part because he stutters. He does not use drugs and he also seems to have a sixth sense about danger. If he feels something is off, or going wrong, he instantly kills the other person. He is willing to murder and supervise kidnappings but he is not one of the cartel's professional killers, a sicario. His job is moving drugs.

He operates under the control of Number 12 and also works with Ruben Rodriguez Dorado, a man also known as El Leches, The Milk, often called Leches Tontas—meaning goofy. The nickname describes his nature—he is a mama's boy, a wimp, a kind of clumsy fool. His wife lives on the US side but often she boots him out for not making enough money in his work, and then he goes home to his mother in Juárez. Sometimes he and Picus work together on shipments. The organization is divided into cells in order to control information. These cells rub up against each other on various assignments, and then drift apart. So Picus and Leches are not partners but people who from time to time associate with each other on loads. Number 12 in turn works under the control of two superiors and they report to their boss who reports directly to Don Vicente.

Gonzalez is a minor thing until the death of Number 12, just one of a legion of hired hands the Juárez organization uses to move drugs into the US. His value lies in his legitimate business ties to the US that enable him to cross the bridge into El Paso without raising any suspicions in US Customs. But he is a throwaway person, one easily replaced. If he had continued personally running loads, he would inevitably have lost one. Then, he would likely have been executed. The money is very good in the drug industry but almost no one ever makes it to retirement. But when Number 12 dies there is confusion. People like Picus are left floating. He cannot get work. He has lost his niche in the machine called the Juárez organization.

He eventually becomes an underling of Pedro Sanchez, a man known as El Tigre. Sanchez comes from nothing and begins his career as a car thief. In the course of his work, he learns all the back roads. Then he advances to moving shipments of drugs for the cartel. His deep knowledge of the regional geography makes him a genius at avoiding any kind of checkpoint. Even in a drug industry with bribed cops and officials, there is always an air of piracy. Nothing can be certain when a cargo has so much value. The ultimate security lies in trusting no one.

Sanchez, El Tigre, is a tranquil man and very good to the people who work for him. He buys them houses and is seen by the poor in the campo as a Robin Hood. He is never rowdy and needs very few bodyguards. The poor become his eyes and ears. He likes to keep a space between him and the world and makes it known he does not favor being mentioned in *narcocorridos*. He is very protective of his people and to defend them "he would put his hands in the fire," a member tells me. When he moves drugs through the villages, he scatters a lot of money around and so whole towns love him.

He is also very loyal to the boss, except when defending his people, and if ordered to kill he always obeys. Sanchez recruits poor guys from the campo and they are very hard and can sleep on the ground in the cold of the Sierra. Like many people in the business, he accumulates nicknames. Besides El Tigre, he is called The Sun, The Father. And Burner of Earth.

Sanchez moves up and he teams with El Grande as the two men helping to control the plaza, the crossing in Juárez. The division of labor works this way: one man, Sanchez, takes care of shipping the drugs, the other man, El Grande, maintains control of the crossing by bribing police and government officials and by killing any competitors who try to use the crossing without paying. El Grande is a huge man, tall, heavy and very intelligent. He has his people learn computers and electronic eavesdropping. He has all the frequencies for the police forces. Both report to someone above them who in turn reports to Don Vicente. But now they are men of power.

It is difficult to wrap one's mind around such power or the sums it entails. Sanchez is moving loads of thirty or forty tons of marijuana. And when he brings the money back from the US, this means shipments of thirty or forty million dollars in cash. Within this fabric, Picus rises and soon teams up with an old friend, Chullin, Jesus Aguayo Salas, who comes from the same area of Chihuahua. Sanchez likes their work and so they rapidly progress to bigger shipments. Picus builds a large trucking company to move the drugs, move the money and launder the money. Together, they suddenly move from small smugglers to men who handle tens of millions for the organization.

Here is how it works—Picus and Chullin deal with ten clients, and these clients are selected by the organization. Each client must buy at least a half ton of marijuana a week. The clients only know their contact, Picus or Chullin, and Picus and Chullin only know their ten clients. The system is a series of compartments and if someone is arrested or is a traitor, the damages can be limited by this control on information.

But nothing is ever stable. From the outside, it looks like a perfect machine of money, drugs and power. From the inside, it is nothing but insecurity and change. For example, Leches shifts and is assigned to El Grande. And El Grande shifts to another state and JL, José Luis Ledesma, takes over with Sanchez as co-operator of the plaza.

JL, also known as Two Letters, El Loco and The Beast, is

cold and intelligent. He takes over the plaza in silence. For two months, JL does nothing but watch. He is known as a man who keeps his eyes open and his mouth closed. He fires all the local bosses. He buys a lot of Chihuahua—the mayors, the media, the cops. He kills easily. Nothing moves without paying him and in turn, this means paying Don Vicente. The fee is so much a kilo and under JL's leadership thirty or forty trucks arrive in the city in caravans.

Picus, with his growing trucking company, works for Sanchez and has two tasks: to move tons of drugs across the bridge into stash houses in El Paso and to move tens of millions of dollars back across the bridge into Juárez. Think of him as a successful middle manager, a man making millions but still a man who takes orders from people above him. And his career is based on successful shipments. If he starts losing loads, then he becomes a question mark to his superiors. And if these losses continue, he is killed because the surest way to insure loyalty is to murder anyone suspected of being a traitor.

Picus and Chullin run a half-ton load into El Paso in 2005. Fine. Then the load is captured. This is a problem but not fatal. Then the lost load is reported as being a hundred pounds. Now there is a serious problem: what became of the other nine hundred pounds? Both Picus and Chullin say they delivered the full weight. But if that is true, then why was this small amount reported in the newspaper?

An explanation must be found. And so, Picus and Chullin are invited home. In this case, home is a safe house in a city that is not Juárez, a place where cartel members gather to enjoy life and feel free of stress for a brief spell. Such a place does not arouse fear in them. There are safe houses and death houses. If one is told to meet at a death house, a place where people are tortured, murdered and then buried in the patio, there is always some anxiety because a person never knows if he is invited to do the killing or to be killed. I once interviewed a person who belonged to a cell of ten people. He was told to come to a death house and meet with another cell of ten people. Only when he arrived did he learn to his relief that his cell was to execute the other cell.

In this instance, Picus and Chullin went to the safe house without being forced. It was a favored place in a gated community. The house had ten bedrooms, four living rooms and was surrounded by a thirty-foot wall. There is a room full of pool tables, $25,000 apiece. A fifty-foot bar stocked with fine liquor. Paintings on the wall and a kitchen that runs day and night. Women are abundant—they come for the good times— and the bedrooms are busy. There are cameras everywhere monitoring all activity. When the boss takes a woman to bed, the camera in his room is shut down and armed guards bar the door. In back is a pool and garden. And hidden inside the building is a secret room with no visible door and this is stocked with a thirty-day supply of food and water. If danger descends, the boss disappears into this chamber. On the big wooden front door is carved a simple declaration—*Carrillo Fuentes*.

Picus and Chullin come happily. Everyone in the house, forty or fifty men, is armed. When Picus and Chullin arrive their guns are seized. Not because the others fear them but to prevent one from killing the other in order to avoid betrayal. They are taken to the office and grilled by fifteen men. Picus begins to stutter, Chullin is calm. Both deny stealing the missing nine hundred pounds of the load.

Their boss, Pedro Sanchez, wants to wait, investigate and then decide their fates. El Grande is brought back for this investigation because of his earlier history with Picus when he was promoted. He recommends a cautious path— kill both Picus and Chullin in order to be sure of getting the traitor. But Sanchez and El Grande finally agree to wait and look into matters. Picus and Chullin are chained in separate rooms. Messages fly back and forth to El Paso where a lawyer is commissioned to investigate.

The days crawl by, one by one. The house is noise, women, drink, cocaine and the whirr of faxes. Leches is there watching it all. He has come to the house in part because he likes a good party. But also because he constantly monitors rumors on the street.

Leches lives up to his nickname. If sent to do a kidnapping he often fucks up and goes to the wrong address. If sent on a murder assignment, he tends to think too much about what he is to do and thus stumbles rather than glides toward a sound execution. He talks a lot and comes across as a fool. He drinks a lot. Logically, he would have been killed long ago for incompetence. But he has a singular merit—he can socialize anywhere. He haunts bars, parties and discos, he has a patter, he boozes heavily. And he never seems to forget a single thing he hears. He has useful ears and eyes for the organization and this keeps him alive.

Juárez is crowded with spies. The taxi driver, the bartender, the whore, the waiter, an army of snitches reporting to the organization. Over the years, I have witnessed people drop to a whisper within their own homes when talking of the drug world. The daily papers go weeks and months and never print the name of Don Vicente.

Once I drank in the bar of the country club where Don Vicente keeps a house. I started making notes and my Mexican friend became nervous. I ignored him. Next, he nudged me and pointed out that the bartender was suddenly on the phone. So we left.

I walked across the tiled lobby under a fine dome and as I descended the steps outside, an unmarked state police car with two cops out of uniform suddenly pulled in and the men stared at me with hard eyes.

That is the fact of the city—nothing is visible to the eye

and yet there is the sense that everything is being watched. It can all look benign. I tracked the history of an execution once. It was planned in fine bars in Juárez and a Starbucks in El Paso. In the end, the victim was buried in the backyard of a condo in a good neighborhood a few blocks from a Radisson hotel and sushi bar.

Chullin and Picus wait for days. The lawyer in El Paso discovers that the original police document has only a hundred pounds seized, but the court documents have the full half ton. Logically, this explains the question of the shipment. The two leaders, Sanchez and El Grande, go back and forth on what should be done. Grande still leans toward killing them as the cleanest solution. But Sanchez is stubborn, his entire history is sticking up for his people.

A compromise is finally reached. Chullin is told to keep an eye on Picus. And Dorado, El Leches Tontas, is told to spy on both of them and write a report every week.

There is a sense of suspended death in this decision. El Grande suspects Picus but decides that letting him go may lead to finding other traitors in the organization. The Juárez organization in the past had a simple rule—if a load was lost, everyone connected with that load died in order to be sure of stopping betrayal. But since the death of Amado Carrillo, there has been a softening and so both men are freed, or more accurately released until it becomes clear who should die.

There is a sense that neither man can really flee. Chullin has a US record from that load he lost with Picus and can no longer legally cross. Picus also has a record now and has had his crossing documents revoked by the US, but he has also amassed a great deal of money and now owns a transport company with ninety semis. He is a rich man. He moves tens of millions across the bridge from El Paso to Juárez for El Tigre, Pedro Sanchez.

Surely, such a vested man will not bolt. And if he falters,

if he starts preparations for flight, well, El Leches, Dorado, is watching his every move.

So the party ends, the men go free, and there is nothing to do but wait until the traitor becomes apparent.

Loads continue to be seized by US agents and clouds of suspicion grow around Picus. El Leches files his weekly reports. In May 2008 Pedro Sanchez is arrested in southern Chihuahua which raises a suspicion that there must be a traitor in the organization.

But by then Picus has vanished. He disappears from sight in March 2008. He has prepared an exit from his dilemma by tipping off ICE about loads crossing into the US—loads that are taken down by ICE in distant cities like Chicago to draw attention away from their snitch. He moves to El Paso and continues to advise ICE. He has traded one death trap for another. Logically, he should take his money and his family and vanish deep into the heart of the United States. But now he is a slave of ICE, and they keep him in El Paso where he works for them. In many ways, DEA and ICE have the same ethic as the organization—they use informants as throwaway items and do not concern themselves with the danger this creates.

It is hard to know when Picus starts working with ICE. He is taken to the safe house and interrogated sometime in 2005, and he dies in May 2009. He flees to El Paso in March 2008, most likely because he could hear footsteps. Clearly, if ICE wanted to keep him safe, they would have moved him far from El Paso. His presence there suggests they needed him close to Juárez. Loads keep being lost. And yet Picus does two things—he keeps phoning his friend Chullin. And he keeps working, moving money south and drugs north. But he does this by phone and keeps his whereabouts a secret from the organization. The more interesting point is the fact that he lives with his family, visits relatives and still cannot be found by the organization. Chullin has made himself scarce out of fear for his life. He has many businesses in Chihuahua, and knows the ground like the back of his hand. He is a man who can melt into the vast countryside and he does.

Leches can cross, but has no idea where to look for Picus.

Picus opens his businesses, trucking companies and the like, in El Paso. His neighbors find him a quiet family man who arouses no suspicions. In part he benefits from the collapse in Juárez due to violence and recession. Given this disarray, a prosperous businessman from Juárez can recreate himself in El Paso and be relatively unnoticed. Picus is almost invisible in this new wave of refugees.

His wife continues to go back to Mexico under the assumption that she is exempt from any problems with his activities. She sometimes visits family in Villa Ahumada, the town where her husband's people are in the cheese business. She makes friends with the neighbors in her El Paso neighborhood and tends to her children.

Then one day she travels to Villa Ahumada and does not return.

She has been snatched by the organization in the belief that Picus will have to surface to rescue her. But he does not rise to the bait.

So they cut off one of her fingers and have it delivered to a relative. Picus does nothing. They cut off another finger and deliver it. Still, he makes no response. Then, they cut off a third finger. He remains unreachable.

Eventually, they let her go. This happens in late 2008.

A neighbor visits her in an El Paso hospital and she explains that she lost her fingers in an accident. But she does not elaborate on how this happened.

Once there were pretensions of one's family being out of bounds—though this is half fantasy. In the nineties, one member in Sinaloa had his wife's head delivered to him in a hatbox. But still, there was a sense that families would generally be spared. Now this is ending.

The president of Mexico, Felipe Calderón, keeps escalating his official war against the drug industry and eventually has at least forty-five thousand soldiers fanning out across the country. There is talk of a war between Beltran Leyva and Chapo Guzman in Sinaloa and between Chapo Guzman and the Juárez organization and between everyone and the Zetas who have taken over the killing for the Gulf organization. There is talk that Chapo Guzman dines in Juárez. There is talk that Chapo Guzman meets with JL, the key man under Vicente Carrillo. There is talk by the US agencies that violence may spill across the border. Rick Perry, the governor of Texas, sends his Rangers to the line.

Picus can cross the river, buy a house, start businesses and still the organization has trouble finding him. Just as he can be a traitor, tip US officials to loads and yet it takes time before the organization can even decide that he is a traitor. The DEA produces charts of the organizations with boxes and lines, a pyramid of power. On the charts, the drug industry looks as tightly knit as a Fortune 500 company. But on the ground, it resembles a cluster of affinity groups, gangs, that hook up for deals, then float away from each other. I have known too many informants who operated beneath the radar of the drug organizations even as they gave up loads and earned big checks from the US government for these routine betrayals. I once lunched with a man who regularly partied in Mexico with the leadership of the Gulf organization and just as regularly reported to law enforcement in the US.

So Picus flees and moves from one web to another. The border zone of the United States and Mexico lacks privacy. Electronic surveillance, though officially denied, is normal. I once looked into a murder on the line with a retired DEA agent. He would not use his cell phone until we were close to a hundred miles from the line. He said he knew they listened because he had seen the transcripts. Phone calls, the Internet, everything is sucked up and sorted through. People in the drug industry cope by speaking in constantly shifting codes, or never speaking of business on the phone at all. In 2004, a death house was revealed in Juárez that had run five months and killed at least a dozen people, some US citizens.

The two agencies despise each other. DEA resents ICE's efforts to work on drug cases since this cuts into DEA's business. All ICE drug operations must be authorized by DEA but that hardly means that ICE keeps DEA informed on how the case is unfolding. On the border, no one trusts anyone. Agencies don't trust fellow agencies, agents often don't trust fellow agents. Everything is about making cases, taking bribes and advancing.

Picus moves and burrows in. After his wife loses her three fingers, he relocates again in April 2009, into a two-story house of over three thousand square feet with a pool in the backyard. He has businesses with listings, but they use his home address. And yet he has money. He knows he is hunted because he has done such hunting. He knows the caliber of people who will come for him because he has worked with them.

He is losing his survival skills. Or he finds his skills now useless. He continues to visit his relatives in the El Paso area, apparently because he trusts them. In the drug business, trust is the first step toward death.

I hear these voices. They say their partner has their back. They say they can't trust anyone. They say in the end you must trust someone and in the end you die. Out there, on the street, in the deserts, under the bridges at midnight where no light can penetrate, in those places you must take the chance and no matter what you do to reduce the odds, no matter how smart you are, no matter how tough and good with blades, there is the moment you must trust someone to watch your back and that is the moment, the window, the little crack in the universe, where your death will slip through with the silence of a blade on the throat, the speed of a bullet through the brain.

This is never written. The people who talk the good book don't want to know these chapters and verses.

On May 15, Picus visits some relatives and goes about various errands in the city. The same day, Leches also visits the same relatives, keeps watch on the house, and follows Picus home. That evening the El Paso chief of police is standing in his backyard when he hears some shots. At the same time, Picus has just parked his truck and is walking toward his home when he takes eight rounds and dies.

At first, the reaction in the US press is that a businessman has been slain. Then, that a lieutenant of the Juárez organization has been killed in the US and this is unprecedented. Experts weigh in and fear this is the opening shot of a bloodbath that will spill across the border.

And then the lid blows.

First, it is discovered that a soldier, eighteen-year-old US Army Pfc. Michael Jackson Apodaca from Ft. Bliss, was the triggerman. Two other local teenagers helped with driving and surveillance. They split a $10,000 payment. Then it is discovered—to the anger of the police chief—that Picus is an informant for ICE and has regularly been tipping them to loads of drugs, which would imply he still had connections with the cartel. Then it is discovered that the man directing the hit, El Leche, Ruben Rodriguez Dorado, is also a member of the organization and an informant for ICE.

The details spill out. How ICE warned Picus to be careful because someone was trying to get into his cell phone account in order to learn where he lived. Of course, ICE did not mention that Leches Dorado, their own informant, was the person on his trail. And there is a fair chance they did not know that the agents running Leches did not know that Picus was also an ICE informant. Just as the agents running Picus likely did not know the man seeking to kill him was also an ICE informant.

And then a silence as ICE announces they cannot comment on pending matters.

As for the members of the organization, they are stunned for two reasons. First, they assumed even if Picus were killed in the shootout he would most likely take Leches with him since he was far more competent and ruthless. Second, while they felt Picus was most likely a traitor, they never knew that Leches worked for ICE until the newspaper published the fact after the killing.

When Picus is shot, his wife, the woman with three fingers severed, calls 911. Then she calls ICE. Then she takes the kids and leaves and has not been seen since.

And everything goes back to normal. Picus and his death become a forgotten detail in 2010, a year when 2,657 people die in Juárez—sixty-six of them cops. Thirteen die in El Paso. The US continues to promote its War on Drugs. The president of Mexico continues to promote his War on Drugs. People continue to die. Picus and his story go away.

The man stops speaking, his tale floats in the air. He knows it will never connect with anything, not with walls, not with tens of thousands of agents on the line, not with national security. Not with Jericho. No, with nothing. The story is now weightless, like so many things on the line. They happen, they are ignored or they are the source of lies. They are noises, not voices, and so the stories become garbled and shape changers and piles of dead Mexicans mean that violence is crossing the line.

It is quiet now. He is done. He says, ah, we have people in your agencies. He says the story of Picus is nothing since neither he nor his killer matter. They are simple little hands that move tens of millions at a time and when they die other hands appear and nothing changes, nothing at all.

That is the beauty of a culture of fear. Men die, women get their fingers cut off but nothing matters except the fear and nothing can end the fear, ever. With time the fear expands beyond the walls and the walls are never enough because there is the matter of Jericho and the horns and the walls tumbling down.

The man now sits there silently with a soft smile. His world rolls on and on, unnoticed. The walls and the rest, they are props for someone else. They do not figure in his tales.

PART IV

Jericho

Joshua started out as a spy himself. God honored betrayal in the olden times. Joshua was Egyptian-born and started out as the right-hand man of Moses—even went partway up Mount Sinai with him when he climbed the peak to fetch the Ten Commandments. When Moses died, Joshua announced he been picked by him as his successor. Besides these management skills, he was good on the killing ground. Jericho was just one of his slaughters—he even asked God to make the sun and moon stand still so he'd have a longer day for his killing at Gibeon. But this time he didn't kill everybody, instead making them slaves who had to cut wood and carry water. God actually helped out at this battle by tossing down some big hailstones that killed more people than the Israeli spears.

He was an early enemy of walls, at least if they kept him from killing people.

And it came to pass, when Joshua had spoken unto the people, that the seven priests bearing the seven trumpets of rams' horns passed on before the LORD, and blew with the trumpets: and the ark of the covenant of the LORD followed them. And the armed men went before the priests that blew with the trumpets, and the rereward came after the ark, the priests going on, and blowing with the trumpets. And Joshua had commanded the people, saying, Ye shall not shout, nor make any noise with your voice, neither shall any word proceed out of your mouth, until the day I bid you shout; then shall ye shout. So the ark of the LORD compassed the city, going about it once: and they came into the camp, and lodged in the camp. (Josh. 6:8–11)

When he is an old man and dying, he calls the elders of his nation together and tells them how God has aided him and them in driving away other people and taking the land of other people. And if the Israelis ever intermarry with these people they have killed and robbed and enslaved and driven off, well, then God will take their stolen land back and ruin them.

So he wasn't really against walls at all, just against barriers that got between him and the people he intended to murder.

*　　*　　*

Hot, no clouds.

One black hawk called on a limb and then he lifted, swooped over me screaming. Saw four gray hawks, one on the wing, three perched, climbed the hill above the white house for sale near town. Walked twelve miles and when I returned there was a host of raven voices over the roasted chicken I'd placed out back for them.

I have walked ninety-two miles in nine days. Most of it with a twenty-five-pound pack.

I leave for a story on a border.

I promise myself I will continue doing this each day.

I know I am lying to myself but it seems I must say this lie in order to leave this place. I have sworn off my life for the cry of a hawk, the flash of a wing, the feel of the hills as I pound up and down them with a pack. I spend money I will never have to get binoculars I cannot live without and suddenly the eye gleams, the feathers have fine detail and the beak is polished death on the raptor.

The Cranes

I yearn for some sky. One group of sandhill cranes flies from Siberia to northern Mexico each year making a round trip of fourteen thousand miles. The birds can knock down two to three hundred miles a day, and with the luck of a good tailwind have had five hundred–mile days. They use thermals to rise up into the heavens and Asian cranes have been seen riding above Mount Everest.

They violate all borders in the sky and rigorously enforce them on the ground. Each bird insists on its space—basically, pecking distance when feeding or roosting. Pairs define a sphere around them and a male can become inflamed if it is violated. On the nesting grounds in Canada, Alaska or Siberia, at least sixty acres are policed and the same ground used by the same pair year after year. Young birds seeking to mate must first find ground and given the requirements of proper nesting sites and feeding areas that often means they must wait for their elders to die before they can start their own dynasty.

After a year, a new sandhill crane is evicted by its parents and joins a flock of other juveniles for several years of wandering. At three or four, mates are sought, territory marked out and defended and for a sandhill the world begins again.

There is no government, only a nation.

Falcon Lake

A common black hawk flies over Doug's boat. He rests in the water about three hundred yards from the drowned church that the Hartleys visited. He's cautious. Today he does not wish to go closer—there are two many pangas in the area that could cut him off and ask for money. On Falcon Lake, a kind of feel for things is necessary. If the pangas are out fishing, well, that means things are okay. If they suddenly leave, well, that means something is going down, maybe a drug shipment, and it is best to move off and fish elsewhere.

"If I fish for ten days," Doug explains, "nine of them are here."

The Hartley family held a memorial for David on the lake about ten days after he vanished. They went out with law enforcement to a point on the US side and dropped a wreath in the water. Doug hauled in a television crew and parked on the Mexican side so they could film the event. The television correspondent stared at Tiffany Hartley and kept muttering, "Look at that lying bitch."

Doug was taken aback.

A man has vanished, a woman speaks, politicians talk of this vanishing and on Falcon Lake men continue catching large bass and moving shipments of marijuana.

It no longer matters what happened on Falcon Lake, it may never have mattered.

Killing Ground

The men stand on slick floors amid the screams of dying beasts. The air is blood and the aroma of cooking dead animals. The stockyards are also dying. It is the early 1950s and the killing ground is ebbing away from Chicago. First, the slaughterhouses move off onto the prairies and the plains and then the jobs move into new brown hands.

But always the place is for others, not our kind. The packing plants swallowed generations of Poles and other migrants, and the black men came fleeing Jim Crow and joined in the murder of beasts. I stand on the killing floor, there is a screech of chains as pulleys move carcasses, men hack at bodies and the morning light streams into the plant. I am eight, I smell blood, see entrails spill out, hear the squeals of doomed creatures, watch men with large muscles maneuver forms suddenly emptied of life.

I am on a Cub Scout outing. I am learning my city. I am learning work. I am learning death. The den mother officially guiding us has horror in her eyes. She has brought us to where the money is made but no one ever told her how the money screams where it is made.

Now the yards have gone still. First, you could make more money from the screams if you moved the killing closer to the farms and fields and farther from the unions that demanded higher wages and safe working conditions. My kin took those jobs and so the killing returned to the American-born. Then it was learned you could make more money if you cut the wages in half and hired illegal men from Mexico and Central America and hid from unions and tossed away those who lost an arm or a hand or fingers on the killing ground. Dodge City, Kansas, and other places became Mexican villages where animals died, men were maimed and money screamed.

But I am in the slaughterhouse. Black men kill, animals sway past, hanging off hooks, outside barrels of pickled meat block the horizon, the light is golden, falling from heaven, the bodies keep swinging past, the screams never end, the look in the woman's eyes is horror, they never look at us, they are busy killing and cutting and they are other, they are other colors and other languages and they are how the money is made, then, now, always.

They are what walls are about and why walls fall.

Delta

He dressed in khaki like some apparition out of the veldt. He came to the lower Rio Grande as a high school exchange student in the long ago and then he returned to his Africa. But the place became too hard with the long history between blacks and whites. He could no longer shoulder the bill, face the matter in the morning noon and night and so he migrated, a white man, crossing borders and settling on a border because that was legal, his papers in order, and his money was that good.

There is a price for crossing lines and for maintaining lines. Long ago, I thought of settling in Mississippi because of the beauty of the morning light and the pleasant languor of the people in both speech and movement. The purr of the slow rivers caught my ear. But I could not bear the fact that race entered into every decision every moment of every day. I thought my life would go down in this undertow and I would never be strong enough to swim back to the surface and the golden light of dawn. And of course, the great river, the Mississippi, almost always out of view behind the levees still flowed through the mind day and night.

The man in khaki is very bright and has sad eyes. Our talk begins with birds, a shared passion, then turns to Mexicans—this other great river, the Rio Grande, flows seven miles south through scrub forest, heat and humidity. The talk comes back to whites and blacks in South Africa and inside my head I return to Mississippi.

I think it is the small country churches, little white buildings with small steeples out on dirt lanes where poor black people gather on Sunday morning for services that seem endless to me and gospel swells of song that rise like giant waves and roll over the flat land. The shouts of the deacon leading the hymns, the smell coming through the windows from the plowed ground. That beckoned me.

But I could not do it and returned to the Mexican border. There are lines and then there are lines. And on the Mexican border race was never a line for me. Language, culture, yes, lines in a way. But race was like the new American wall, huge and hard and unyielding.

I look at the man in khaki with his sad eyes.

Falcon Lake

They are at Guerrero Viejo taking pictures of the church that has reemerged from the lake because of drought. Then they get on their jet skis and leave. As they round a point they see a boat off to the side and the people on the boat wave in a friendly manner.

They snap some more photographs and when they are about halfway to the US border, Tiffany can only guess the location she says, they see three boats coming toward them—the pangas favored by Mexican fishermen and Mexican drug smugglers. The Hartleys cut through them and then the pangas turn around and begin chasing them and the shooting begins. Tiffany sees two shots hit the water on her left. She looks back and sees her husband has been thrown off his ski and is in the water facedown. She goes back to check on him. He has been shot in the head and seems lifeless. She tries to pull him onto her jet ski but fails. She is petite; he is six foot and 250 pounds.

A boat comes up, a gun is pointed at her but nothing is said. And then the boat leaves. She continues to try and get her husband on her ski but she sees the three boats coming back and she flees and leaves David behind. They continue to shoot at her but she rides on the side of the ski with the craft between her and her attackers.

She pulls up to a house on the US side, asks the man for his cellphone, calls 911. On the recording of that call, she sounds like a woman who has just witnessed the slaughter of her husband.

Almost instantly there are doubts about the story given by Tiffany Hartley.

No panga could ever chase a jet ski.

No one can figure out why Mexicans would murder a US citizen and then let a witness escape.

Some are puzzled why she keeps saying her story is a story rather than saying she is telling what happened. She appears very calm in many television interviews, and fails to cry sufficiently for many viewers.

Her jet ski is unmarked despite the shots fired at her.

She is not covered with blood though later a speck of her husband's blood is found on her life vest.

She insists she simply wants her husband's body back and is not interested in finding who killed her husband and trusts in an ultimate justice.

The body is not found.

The jet ski is not found.

The Mexican comandante investigating the case expresses his doubt that the incident ever happened.

Then his head is delivered to his department in Ciudad Miguel Alemán in a suitcase.

Some explain the day away by saying the Hartleys got into a drug deal that went bad.

No evidence is ever offered.

Some explain the day away by saying the Hartleys were murdered by Zetas because they threatened a shipment of drugs across the lake.

No evidence is ever offered.

Following the disappearance of David Hartley there are no more incidents on Falcon Lake. Tiffany Hartley maintains

a website, BringDavidHome.com, and speaks out about violence spilling across the border.

The lakes are bone-dry.

The Cranes

There is no stopping the dance. They dance for joy, they dance for love, they dance for mates, they dance for practice, they dance alone, they dance as pairs, they dance as flocks with thousands of sandhills twirling, leaping, tossing sticks and grass in the air. Sometimes they dance predators away from a nest. They dance for no reason at all that anyone can discern.

There can be no end to the dance.

It is life to a sandhill crane.

There is the bow, the run-flap, the ground-stab, the jump, the wing-spread-hold, the wing-spread-forward-tilt, the jump-rake, the straight-leg highstep, the object-toss, the stab-grab-wave. Sometimes one bird dances around another, sometimes pairs dance. They perform jump-turns, minuets, salutes and the run-flap-glide. They do the single-wing-spin, the gape and gape-sweep, the curtsey, the tuck-bob, and the arch.

Jericho

I stopped marching.

> And Joshua rose early in the morning, and the priests took up the ark of the LORD. And seven priests bearing seven trumpets of rams' horns before the ark of the LORD went on continually, and blew with the trumpets: and the armed men went before them; but the rereward came after the ark of the LORD, the priests going on, and blowing with the trumpets. And the second day they compassed the city once, and returned into the camp: so they did six days. (Josh. 6:12–14)

I stopped marching a long time ago. For years, while the wall was being built and celebrated on the US border I said nothing and did nothing. I felt in my nation's culture of fear the wall was inevitable.

I looked at the wall and knew that I hated all walls, even the ones around my house.

I walk the creek, feel the breeze on my face, hear a gray hawk cry from the top of a cottonwood. Things flow together, the waters rise and flood the land, the rains stay away and the ground burns, the day buries other days and I stand on thousands of years of spent appetites and ruined dreams.

Nothing seems to stop these beginnings and endings.

The hawk lifts off the tree and the hunt begins.

The Butcher

A storm broods on the mesa in the trough of a Sunday afternoon. The street runs black and silent since the repaving a week ago took away the rumbles. The lawyer sits on the brown leather couch and is about to explode. He was in the jailhouse visiting a client and then he came down the elevator and somehow in the lobby he ran into a guy.

And then it happens.

But it is not that simple. The guy he'd gone to see was a gang member nailed by immigration and waiting for his deportation. His girlfriend was wrapping up a degree in criminology and wanted to keep her guy on this side of the fence. The lawyer listened and said he'd see what he could do. His practice was preparing people for a slow death. Immigration courts are a backwater of the federal justice system, a place where a low hum buzzes in the heads of the barely awake judges, political hacks put out to pasture in a place where they can't pester citizens and have to use their small knives on foreigners.

The voices are low in such courtrooms, the cases done by rote, husbands trying to reunite with wives, wives with husbands, dates whispered out—always far in the future, and the hope is everyone will go away and leave the court alone.

The clerk is fat, the judge fifty-something and finished with the ambitions of life. The walls paneled, lights fluorescent and the petitioners sit in rows numbed by the slow movement through the docket. Out the windows, the sun shines on a world that hardly knows of such a room.

The clerk reads the case title.

The judge scans his schedule, tosses out some distant date.

The petitioner and counsel mumble their agreement.

So he is leaving the jailhouse after half-listening to a client when this guy comes out of the elevator and says, "Hey, you're a lawyer, right?"

He stops, sees a Mexican guy in his late twenties weighed down with tattoos. He reaches in his pocket and hands the guy a card. And moves on.

The next day, Saturday, the guy shows up. Turns out he's been there before—the lawyer's secretary remembers him.

Now he's back.

The lawyer is busy, packed in an office for forty-five minutes with other clients. The guy waits, sprawled on a chair in the lobby surrounded by paintings of illegal Mexicans trying to punch through the river, the wall, and the armed agents swarming everywhere.

His turn finally comes.

He sits in a chair in the office, the door is open.

The lawyer nods.

The man gets up and closes the door.

He says, "I am called El Carnecero, The Butcher. I want to talk to you about a woman I love."

"Wait a minute," the lawyer sputters, "You're El Carnecero?"

The man smiles.

"Yeah. I run a hundred and twenty-five sicarios in Juárez."

The lawyer exhales. He wants nothing to do with this case.

He looks at El Carnecero and asks, "You're not going to make soup of me if I lose, are you?"

"No, no, no, Señor. Not you. No."

The lawyer sighs.

"Look," El Carnecero continues, "I gotta tell you I don't want you going to Juárez without telling me. It is very dangerous there. Now I am recruiting good-looking girls as sicarias, they can get close to anyone. So don't go picking up any girls, you hear?"

"I don't go to Juárez anymore."

"Ah, very good. And I don't want you down by the bridge anymore, either."

The lawyer snaps alert. At first he can't understand what the man means. And then he remembers having an ad filmed down by the bridge with Mexico in the background, a bit of footage for publicizing his immigration practice.

"No," El Carnecero says, "stay away from the bridge, it is not safe there. People in that area commit crimes. And report to me."

He remembers the row of taxis, the vendors peddling this and that, the feel of the summer sun on his face as he cut the ad, the sense of standing in the US and being . . . immune from over there.

His world has slowly shrunk during the violence. He now has a security system in his house. He has a remote to start his car in case of a bomb. He has a carry permit for a gun. But still, don't go to the bridge in his city to film an ad for his practice because he is being watched?

El Carnecero smiles.

"Let's talk about the case."

It is cut-and-dried. He met a woman and fell in love and then immigration caught her. She was illegal in the US and is now in detention. He wants her free and so he has come to see the lawyer.

"Well, to be freed and not deported she would need to file for political asylum. And to qualify for that she'd have to give evidence that her life is in danger in Mexico because she belongs to a particular social group that cannot be changed, and that this classification means her death. You understand?"

The man takes in the lawyer's statement, and smiles.

"Ah, this will be easy then. Both her uncles have been killed—their heads cut off. My people did it. I could arrange testimony about this, that she is doomed, you know, because of my sicarios. That would work, no?"

The lawyer sees all the doors closing and leaving him trapped with El Carnecero and his case.

He tries another route. "If I take the case, my fee will be $10,000."

"No problem."

The lawyer's heart sinks.

He says, "Even if I get her released, it does not mean she can stay here. It will only mean she is free and on this side until her case comes up and is decided."

El Carnecero stops smiling. His mind seems to shift from being the boss of something to being the prisoner of something.

He says, "I love her. I must have her. Even if she loses, and is expelled to Juárez, well, then I will move there, too, and if they kill us we will die together. This is not a business matter for me."

The lawyer's last hope vanishes. He is dealing with a man possessed and is now chained inside some border story of Romeo and Juliet.

He looks at a tattoo of an eagle on El Carnecero's right wrist.

"What does that mean?"

"Ah, the eagle? It means I am a capo. Sometimes, I must put my hand over it if I am dealing with the wrong people, you know. But that hardly ever happens. I have federal police identification, you know."

And then he leaves.

Two weeks later, the mother of the girl comes by the office. She works in Juárez, in the prison. And she is concerned about her daughter's case and if she can be released from the detention center.

The lawyer asks her, "Do you believe what El Carnecero says about his work?"

She answers, "All I know is that my daughter is afraid of him."

"Yes, but he says he had both her uncles killed and their heads cut off."

"He did? No, no, they killed her distant cousins, not her uncles. Why?"

The lawyer suddenly sees his life returning to him.

A distant relative is not enough to qualify for a filing for political asylum.

So, the next time El Carnecero comes to his office, he tells him he cannot take the case because there is nothing he can do given the actual facts.

For a moment, the lawyer wonders if El Carnecero will order the execution of family members closer to his beloved. But he says nothing and simply leaves.

This is love in this place.

Falcon Lake

Upriver at San Ygnacio, there is an effort to restore an old building from the era of Indian raids with ruins possibly dating back to the 1830s. Frank Briscoe is doing the historical architectural study. He points to a sundial over the main gate. Two brothers, he says, were taken by the Comanches but they escaped and, guided by the stars, made their way back to San Ygnacio. They put up the sundial to always remind them how the heavens had saved them.

He has heard shooting across the river when Mexican gunships have rolled in and wiped out camps of what he assumes are bad guys. But in the main, he is happy to be in San Ygnacio with its core of ancient buildings. The town was supposed to be abandoned when Falcon Lake went in but the locals fought removal and stayed and now they possess the only real structures from the days of Mexico and Spain.

The line lives and the line moves and the line is crossed and the line is erased. The border has shifted over the centuries, violence has crossed the line in both directions. Comanche raiders considered the Spanish settlers at San Ygnacio to be invaders and dealt with them accordingly. Smuggling is as old as the line. Once it was booze. Then it was people. Now drugs come north and money and guns are smuggled south.

Theories cross the line. Sheriff Gonzalez says he has informants he cannot name who say it was drug people who killed David Hartley. A private intelligence firm says it has informants who say Hartley's body was burned and his jet ski cut up and destroyed. The sheriff says he has eyewitnesses who saw Tiffany Hartley being chased across the lake but he cannot name them for security reasons. The Mexican officials doubt the incident ever happened.

The Line

The dust hangs over the valley and the trails start a few hundred miles to the north, trails that lead from the fence into the United States. The village lives off smuggling people. I watch as illegals group for the march north. A truck roars past on the dirt lane. Then another, cutting very close to my machine. Finally, two pickups roll up, one on each side and park so close I cannot open a door. I look over, each truck is full of men. I leave. A small convoy follows me to the border.

The line is hard-edged if you face the law and move people or drugs but it is soft and vague if you are a bird in the sky, a seed floating in the air. The storms also move at will. Guns fire in the night, trucks move without headlights, a chopper hovers and beats on. Sometimes, I can feel death on one side, and not find it on the other. There are those who say this is impossible, that this cannot be, but these same people never wish to explain how one side of the line can stay rich and the other remain poor.

There is a night on the line when the stars storm the heavens at precisely 1:29 a.m. and I hear two bursts of automatic weapons fire, a single shot and then a flurry of five, a single shot then a fast four or five more and I walk around outside and sense the rounds were maybe two or three hundred yards away and I watch the bats careen against the heavens.

Down by the river the agents hide everywhere and wait. Down by the river there is a line in the water and crossing it means life and crossing it means death.

Down by the river I shot my baby and this border is not going to be secure and this guy stands there while I am writing in my notebook and his eyes say I am a crazy person and he says he thinks I am an addict because I will sit there writing as if he does not exist and then I will look up and say something to him and then vanish back into my writing and leave him behind.

They say blood is spilling across the border and a professional killer says I am obsessed and addicted and may need help and the wheel of death keeps spinning south of the river and the cries of death and violence keep rising north of the river and no fact is considered evidence and no claim is dismissed and the bass feed in Falcon Lake and the biggest and oldest, the breeding females, lurk in the deep waters and the statements of the authorities may be repeated but the life of the line is beneath contempt.

The Mexicans are the others, the Canaanites and the breath of the Lord blows against them and they must perish, it is written, or will be written.

I sit at night and stare into the stars because they have watched the lies of walls for thousands of years.

And the stars know they will die and the stars know the wall will come tumbling down.

And I wonder in the gray light of dawn what has happened to us. Not the wars, not the loves, not the drunks or the days toiling. I wonder why we have forgotten where we have been, what made us and what we felt and knew along the way. I wonder why brown faces at the wall frighten us. I wonder who killed the love and drank that last bottle to boot.

We have walls but we have no one left who can feel a wall. Or climb a wall. The others feel the walls and climb the walls and we scorn them. Even the memories are erased or denied. And my God, Carl Sandburg in 1916 pushed "Halsted Street Car" out the door and it roared through the American mind and then somehow was derailed by our schooling and our dying hungers and

Try with your pencils for these crooked faces,
That pig-sticker in one corner—his mouth—
That overall factory girl—her loose cheeks.
Find for your pencils
A way to mark your memory
   Of tired empty faces.
After their night's sleep,
   In the moist dawn
   And cool daybreak,
   Faces
   Tired of wishes,
   Empty of dreams.

And now we are afraid of faces and we no longer ride with a pig-sticker, the loose-cheeked shopgirl, we won't be caught dead in such a ride because it is dangerous. We need a wall, build one plenty high, to reach to the heavens so that the plagues floating in the air are blocked, the rain kept out when unwanted, the sun will bang against it unless permission is asked and the strange faces and twisted ideas inside those skulls will be kept out and we shall fatten within our prison and we shall live in peace in cages and we shall feel no stirrings in our loins or have night thoughts that threaten our days and we shall ride the Limited, those lines Carl Sandberg wrote out as we raced toward our safe nothingness and I wonder why we no longer smell Chicago's Halsted Street from my childhood, a roar of bloods and smells and languages.

The Line

The Mexican border is the vital spot of North America, the place where cultures and life-forms collide and rub against each other. It was created by theft (the Mexican War), is bristling with troops and is the historical mating ground of US free trade policies and the relentless poverty of Mexican workers in US-owned border factories. It has never been secured and barring a miracle, it will never be secured. I have crossed illegally on foot more times than I can recall. It has proven a feeble barrier to millions of Mexican workers and a veritable sieve for drugs.

Down by the river, each spring the killers come north, each fall after a season of slaughter they go south. I stand on the tower and I wait. I am in the Santa Ana National Wildlife Refuge just downstream from Reynosa and McAllen. The brush has ocelot and jaguarundi. Soon they will come, a river of killers—hawks, falcons, kites, all streaming south. They say if you stand on this tower during the migration it is like being surrounded by swarms of bees.

Welcome to no-man's-land. Once it was twenty yards, a strip of sixty feet created by President William McKinley to keep businesses from encroaching on the border and creating solid buildings blocking the enforcement of the changing customs laws. One saloonkeeper kept his cigars on the Mexican side of his establishment to avoid payment and things like this could be tolerated. Lines must be respected except when they are not. The intelligence services swallow up everything transmitted over a sixty-mile swath along the border and no one is officially told this but the agents are leery of saying much of anything until they clear this patch of eavesdropping. There is talk in the wind of a new hundred-mile zone of checkpoints and electronic listening but this also is not discussed, nor are the death squads sent south by one nation into the entrails of another. The drones of course are silent and thus can be ignored. The cold falls down and hammers the frail leaves of summer and many of the birds have brazenly fled south. Now black coffee steams as the sun rises and faint warmth hits the face. On the power pole, a great blue heron waits and then lifts off and flaps away.

Clouds drift up from the Sierra Madre and cross the line.

The Earth tilts, summer drifts south.

I join the birds and the insects and the plagues and the rising temperatures in my contempt for lines and the nations I have left, the nations have no place in no-man's-land and I have gone there to gather up the future and rise to the cold vault of heaven.

El Pastor paints the end of his life. Cuauhtémoc, the Aztec emperor, wears a headdress of feathers and holds an AK-47. And what can I do? Everything is starting to swirl together. I am Chicago by childhood, slaughterhouses and raw stench in alleys and Carl Sandburg wrote,

I WANTED a man's face looking into the jaws and throat
    of life
With something proud on his face, so proud no smash
    of the jaws,
No gulp of the throat leaves the face in the end
With anything else than the old proud look:

Even to the finish, dumped in the dust,
Lost among the used-up cinders,
This face, men would say, is a flash,
Is laid on bones taken from the ribs of the earth,
Ready for the hammers of changing, changing years,
Ready for the sleeping, sleeping years of silence.
Ready for the dust and fire and wind.
I wanted this face and I saw it today in an Aztec mask.
A cry out of storm and dark, a red yell and a purple prayer,
A beaten shape of ashes
     waiting the sunrise or night,
     something or nothing,
     proud-mouthed,
     proud-eyed gambler.

And in the painting his woman holds up his child, an infant
clutching a tiny AK-47. A headstone looms with the date of
El Pastor's death. A giant hand reaches down because humans act out their vanities and ignore the fact that they are
pawns of Satan and creations of God.

Cuauhtémoc was tortured by Cortez in an effort to reveal
the nonexistent horde of Aztec gold. Later, Cortez had him
executed because he feared he might lead a revolt, a decision
that is said to have led to the conquistador's insomnia.

Now Cuauhtémoc returns in Pastor's painting and leads
Mexico to its death, just as he led pre-Columbian Mexico to
its death.

His name means Eagle Stooping or Diving.

The painting is blue green black tan and white and glows
like a flower until you lean forward and feel the clip of rounds
empty into your face.

Jericho

You must lie to be a patriot, and you must be honest to be a traitor. That is how it was in the time of Joshua, the man chosen by Moses to lead his people into the Promised Land. Now Joshua had risen as a spy, one of twelve sent by the Israelis into the Land of Canaan so that the ways of the place could be learned, the weaknesses noted, the populations put to the sword, the borders erased and land stolen. Ands so it came to pass, thanks to two more Israeli spies and the help of a whore called Rahab.

> And it came to pass on the seventh day, that they rose early about the dawning of the day, and compassed the city after the same manner seven times: only on that day they compassed the city seven times. And it came to pass at the seventh time, when the priests blew with the trumpets, Joshua said unto the people, Shout; for the LORD hath given you the city. And the city shall be accursed, even it, and all that are therein, to the LORD: only Rahab the harlot shall live, she and all that are with her in the house, because she hid the messengers that we sent. And ye, in any wise keep yourselves from the accursed thing, lest ye make yourselves accursed, when ye take of the accursed thing, and make the camp of Israel a curse, and trouble it. But all the silver, and gold, and vessels of brass and iron, are consecrated unto

the LORD: they shall come into the treasury of the LORD. (Josh. 6:15–19)

The matter of gold and silver was also attended to.

For those fleeing Mexico and seeking political asylum in the United States a proper reverence for lying is also appreciated. It behooves the refugee, like the whore Rahab and the Israeli spies, to deceive. Or be denied and sent back across the wall to death.

Little things can ruin the chance at asylum—a relative in the drug business, a history of leftist politics, a claim that the Mexican government itself is trying to kill you or your family. There is no clear pattern. Killers can come in, torturers can come in. Anyone can come in that the government likes.

But for those found wanting, the human frailties barring entrance are almost limitless.

Boy in the Green Shirt

He sits at the conference table looking at family photographs, staring into the faces of his dead, brothers murdered by the government. He has no work permit, so he toils secretly at night in a bakery.

The long table glows with dark wood, the windowless walls a light wash of green, and two white boards with cases written in by grease pen. The hum of fluorescent lights overhead, faint purr of the cooling system fighting the baked heat of the day. The chairs now mainly empty as the man fingers old photographs of his dead from old marches, they lead not to a better world but the family burying ground. The nephew is tall, all bone, wears a green T-shirt and jeans. He may be twenty. His voice is flat and under control and his eyes are those of a man several centuries older than his birth certificate indicates. He is answering questions but he is really talking to no one.

I have learned that the wall built to defend my country has made me feel like a man without a country.

I look into the ancient eyes of the boy in the green T-shirt who now also lives in no-man's-land.

———

The lawyer is very successful. But he worries about the grow-ing kidnapping threats in Juárez. His fifteen-year-old son was taken and released.

He files a complaint with the authorities.

He moves his family to El Paso to stay with friends.

He returns briefly to Juárez to close down the house.

They kill him in front of his home.

I am at the bar and the woman who directs the chamber of commerce in Zapata talks about the town she grew up in where everyone went over to shop in Mexico and all was well in the world. She has blond hair and dark worried eyes. But she sings a song I have heard everywhere on the border for decades—that we were one community, that things were fine back then and then the trouble came and we had nothing to do with this trouble, it was inflicted on us by governments or agencies or criminals but as for us, we were innocent and it sure was fine back then. Even the wars then were good.

But now, the woman says, she wants to know what is go-ing on.

I hardly speak anymore, and soon I sense I will no longer feel.

Out the door, drive, park and walk in the hills, throw the bag down, the stars come on and there is a faint night breeze and by dawn the temperature drops into the thirties, the stove fires up, steam floats off the coffee cup, doves skim over the mesquite, and I rise and go back.

There are forces stronger than desire, harder than stone, and relentless.

At midnight vultures move past in the soft rain and this flight in the dark hours remains a mystery. The full moon hides in the clouds. Bats swoop around my head feeding.

Eighteen inches of rain have fallen this year in the canyon.

The ravens return and eat the meat I put out.

I sip coffee in a faint drizzle.

At two a.m. a truck without headlights crosses the creek. It comes from the south, and it is heading north on a dirt track to connect with the US interstate highway system.

Finally, the gray light comes and hummingbirds hit the feeders, a whirring in the air as raindrops fall gently off the leaves.

Someone has been shooting at migrants lately. They report this to the authorities when they are caught. But no one knows who it is or why.

A great blue heron slowly beats by in the early morning light.

They find a dead Mexican at the bottom of a cliff near a lake where I fished as a boy. No one knows if he fell or was pushed.

A cardinal comes to the suet bar.

The ducks fly upstream just after sunrise.

The Cranes

As a boy, I felt trapped by the sight of migrating birds. They lived in a permanent spring and summer and I was caged by place and climate. There are rivers in the sky and birds know these channels and live free.

For years I killed them with rifle and shotgun. This is how birds entered American life. John James Audubon considered it a slow day when he did not slaughter a hundred for his art.

Audubon never quite learned how to tell a whooping crane from a sandhill, and thought the latter must be young whoopers. In 1840, on a hunt, he noted, "I had so fair an opportunity that I could not resist the temptation. I felt confident that I must kill more than one ... I fired. Only two flew up, to my surprise. They came down the pond towards me, and my next shot brought them to ground. On walking to the hole, I found I had disabled seven in all."

That was the beginning of the end for cranes. Once Europeans crossed the Missouri, the grasslands that nurtured cranes were doomed and within a century over 90 percent had been swallowed by modern agriculture. Egg collectors helped with the vast death. Toward the end of the nineteenth century, J. W. Preston found a nest of a whooping crane in Iowa. He later wrote, "The eggs were the first I'd seen and were a rare prize to me. When I approached the nest, the bird, which had walked some distance away, came running back ... trotting awkwardly around, wings and tail spread drooping, with head and shoulders brought level with the water ... then with pitiable mien, it spread itself upon the water and begged me to leave its treasure, which, in a heartless manner, I did not."

On the prairies of southwestern Louisiana, the whooping cranes hid out for a while in the marshes. But there was no real safe place as the violence spilled across the border. Claude Eagleson remembers, "It was beautiful to see them up in the sky, always seven or eight to a bunch, circling and crossing each other like people square dancing. You could hear them for a long way. They'd go down in a sweet potato patch and make a pest of themselves eating sweet potatoes, so people would kill them. They were good to eat—better than a goose—and most people would eat them."

One day in 1918, Alcie Daigle of southwestern Louisiana noticed whooping cranes eating rice that spilled from his threshing machine. He killed all twelve—not that hard since cranes have a habit of standing by a fallen member of the family.

There is a history known to cranes, a history where the vast violence spills across the border, the lines of nations are erased by the plow, the ax, the cannon, the rifle, the shotgun, the poison, the trap. Whooping cranes race toward the lip of extinction, the buffalo almost vanishes, the huge flights of passenger pigeons cease, the rivers begin their slow death, the virgin prairie and virgin forests are devoured by hordes of human beings who are unwanted in their native lands. And who kill the natives they find here—plants, animals and people.

When the killing ended, when the drums fell silent, when beasts vanished from the land, when the earth drank deep of poisons, when the wells begin to sink, then a fear replaced the killing, a fear that others might come and do to the new people what they had done to other living things.

The walls went up, the patrols moved through the night, the checkpoints clotted roads and in the airports people had their bodies invaded before they were allowed to fly.

The cranes danced while the people cowered in their shackles.

Memphis

The man is in the city of New York and talking at Riverside Church. And the man reflects on questions of fairness and justice in American foreign and domestic policy. He concludes that true fairness is not a singular act, like throwing a coin to a beggar. It can only be achieved when men and women finally come to see "that an edifice which produces beggars needs restructuring."

It is April 4, 1967, and Martin Luther King will fall dead in three hundred and sixty-five days.

And the old spiritual comes from slave times and got handed up to us by Lead Belly but it sings itself. I watch Dr. Martin Luther King moving toward his bullet in Memphis and each time I am there I think I should go to the kill site, see that balcony and I never do, no, I never do. For years I have had different reasons and none of them are true. I was in Memphis right after that bullet, driving downriver into the delta of the Mississippi and the blood was hardly dry, that anger seething in southern eyes at my Yankee voice and this was a time when the migration still flowed, the people streaming north to escape poverty and lynchings and yet the black towns of the delta clung to some life, Rosedale rang with juke joints, Mound Bayou fattened off burial insurance and in Ruleville on the back lanes speakeasies with ancient piano players and easy women lived on and on, fried chicken in the air, velvet nights of steam heat on the two-lane highways, the flies buzzing and mosquitoes along the river rising from the sloughs, the lights of barges and always the tug of the earth, the bottomless soil of the delta laid down as treasure by the Mississippi.

An old woman wearing a kerchief peeks out the door of her shack at a white man from up north loitering by her wood pile. Twice I heard King preach and now he is dead and the delta with its miseries is a world I do not know and have barely glimpsed.

Now I am in Memphis on one of my trips to the delta and a world is ending and a world is beginning. King's blood is hardly dry and all this because a man who goes by the name of Eric Galt has fled to Mexico after breaking out of a Missouri prison, and in Mexico, like so many Americans, he goes to the whores and then stuffs the inner tube of his spare tire with marijuana. It is the fall of 1967, and he heads north spilling violence across the borders, some drugs too, and he is on a long ride but it will take him to Memphis come April and he'll pull the trigger and shoot Martin Luther King dead. I'll ride through on my way to the delta and the blood is hardly dry and there is nothing to fear from the authorities, they face other demons. And so blood spills north, marijuana comes north, and the word goes out to watch the borders and a bullet launches into a man standing on the balcony of a black motel in Memphis and a few days later I roll through in a car driven by a woman with Vermont plates and there is anger in the air. Beale Street is not a song but a dirge and I am alive to the air streaming through the car window and I am alive to the blank faces of black people as they face the slaughter of a leader in an uncaring white world and I am alive to the brown muscle of the river roiling just beyond the levee.

Like everything that matters and everyone that matters, the death starts with garbage. How do I explain this to myself? I saw three great egrets booming white by the river today, a hawk wheeled overhead, a northern harrier swept soft over the river meadow, a shrike sat lonesome on a branch and the blues of Memphis were back, ringing in my head and James Earl Ray comes north out of Mexico, comes with grass and anger and gets that gun, says he is Eric Galt and the crack of the rifle, the fall, all that, it returns to me. The exact moment it happened I was in Wisconsin staring out at a lake, hosting a party, wine everywhere, candles burning, cheap food smeared on lips, the radio blaring and then this announcement, a shooting down there in Memphis, the man down and dead. Later, cities went up in flames, but that night the music stopped. Death. And I am in a car heading south, following the river, going to Memphis and the delta and velvet nights, slow speech, rich vowels, time without end. Dr. King steps out on the balcony, been a hard day's night for him and we swing low sweet chariot "comin' for to carry me home" but I hear the song in my heart and it says:

If you get there before I do,
Comin' for to carry me home,
Tell all my friends I'm comin' too,
Comin' for to carry me home.

King has come because of a garbage strike by men who tote those cans and for once are asking for a little in the way of wages or decency. All this comes to pass when Echol Cole and Robert Walker are crushed by the equipment on February 1, 1968 and then on February 11 a strike is called and by April, Martin Luther King is heading into Mississippi. Against the will of his staff he says yes, yes, he will stop by Memphis and talk to the people about the justice of garbage men wanting a decent wage, and wanting to not be murdered by the gear that compacts all the trash of the city. The families of the dead men lack the money to bury them and one goes into a pauper's grave.

And so Martin Luther King must come to Memphis and James Earl Ray must come to Memphis in the guise of Eric Galt and Robert Johnson, twenty-one years dead, sang it all: "I got to keep movin' / Blues fallin' down like hail."

Galt gets himself a rifle and near Shiloh, the Civil War battlefield that devoured twenty-four thousand human beings in forty-eight hours, he pauses and tests his new gun and Martin Luther King is swinging into Memphis because a machine ate two human beings and no one seemed to care.

The strikers wear big signs that say I AM A MAN and they walk in an uncaring world. Civil rights can sometimes be talked on the Jericho road, but when it comes to poverty, that cuts too deep into the muscle and bone of American beliefs. Martin Luther King is planning to bring a big caravan of poor people to Washington to slap the face of Congress with poverty, and this, too, is forbidden. Voting is one thing, calling the whole game into question is another.

So he comes, and on the bluff by the Mississippi River Martin Luther King finds his famous mountaintop. It is evening and he stands at the pulpit on April 3 and preaches, he runs through one of his standard preacher things, reviewing the history of the world and saying when he would choose to live and it is not the time of the pharaohs and it is not the time of the ancient Greeks, no, no, and not the time of Rome and so he rolls on and decides that if he could just live.

He is tired and yet he is on fire. He wants to live now because he smells freedom in the wind—and that night, killer tornadoes rake Memphis. He says it is no longer a choice between nonviolence and violence—now the decision is between nonviolence and nonexistence. Yes, yes, he is moving, the slow train is coming into the station and my God, suddenly he is at the edge of Canaan staring into Jericho and he memorably says that he has been to the mountaintop and he has seen the promised land. And while "I may not get there with you," he promises that "we, as a people, will get to the promised land!"

And then he returns to the Lorraine Motel. The next day he stood on the balcony and the bullet found him on the Jericho road.

*   *   *

The language of the Bible is blunt about the killing, and does not bother to justify the killing. The killers are with God, the dead are not.

No one and nothing is with God except for the killers, and the whore Rahab and her people.

> And they burnt the city with fire, and all that was therein: only the silver, and the gold, and the vessels of brass and of iron, they put into the treasury of the house of the LORD. And Joshua saved Rahab the harlot alive, and her father's household, and all that she had; and she dwelleth in Israel even unto this day; because she hid the messengers, which Joshua sent to spy out Jericho. And Joshua adjured them at that time, saying, Cursed be the man before the LORD, that riseth up and buildeth this city Jericho: he shall lay the foundation thereof in his firstborn, and in his youngest son shall he set up the gates of it. So the LORD was with Joshua; and his fame was noised throughout all the country. (Josh. 6:24–27)

I think of walking down the dirt road and my foot coming to rest by the head of a diamondback rattlesnake and I pause, the snake's black tongue flicks out, and still I do not move my foot and not because I fear the snake will strike, no, no, because I no longer care.

Something about walls, walls tumbling down, going up, walls deciding what lives and dies. If Jericho is the solution, then I must look into the matter carefully and understand what was the problem.

And yes the people shouted and yes the priests blew those horns and yes.

So the people shouted when the priests blew with the trumpets: and it came to pass, when the people heard the sound of the trumpet, and the people shouted with a great shout, that the wall fell down flat, so that the people went up into the city, every man straight before him, and they took the city. And they utterly destroyed all that was in the city, both man and woman, young and old, and ox, and sheep, and ass, with the edge of the sword. But Joshua had said unto the two men that had spied out the country, Go into the harlot's house, and bring out thence the woman, and all that she hath, as ye sware unto her. And the young men that were spies went in, and brought out Rahab, and her father, and her mother, and her brethren, and all that she had; and they brought out all her kindred, and left them without the camp of Israel. (Josh. 6: 20–23)

I must shout, and I will begin slowly and then it will build and build. In those olden times of slaves, they would gather outside and do a ring shout and the tempo would be slow and with time quicken and the same thing would be said over and over hour after hour and one of these ring shouts that has come down the dusty roads of our lives is

Joshua fit de battle ob Jericho, Jericho, Jericho
Joshua fit de battle ob Jericho
An' de walls come tumblin' down.

And in this version, one that wells up out of American bondage in the early nineteenth century, the story gets turned on its head and it is no longer about Joshua leading the Israelis as they invade Canaan and murder and enslave people, no, no, it is about the possibility of freedom and how to celebrate that possibility while still wearing the master's shackles and hoeing cotton. They shout, moving counter-clockwise, erasing time and going home, back to freedom days, and swing low sweet chariot coming for to carry me home and the feet shuffle, hands clap, hallelujah and the sound and practice comes from before slavery from West Africa and early ministers sought to end the practice and then decided at least they could change the chants and embed the hollers in the Bible. So hymns arose like "Josuha Fit de Battle ob Jericho," everything in the ring shout stays the same including the fact that shouting had nothing to do with it, that the circle could roll on for hours with soft declarations, that it was about movement and tempo and finally, about walls tumbling down.

You may talk about yo' king ob Gideon
You may talk about yo' man ob Saul
Dere's none like good ole Joshua
At de battle ob Jericho.

But out there in the fields and under the trees at night, back in the line of shacks on the plantation the song changed the story from conquest to freedom. Embedded in the American songbook where it lingers like a time bomb as the new American wall rises, and slowly mauls its way across the southern edge of the country lest others come north and taste the freedom.

Up to de walls ob Jericho
He marched with spear in han'

"Go blow dem ram horns," Joshua cried,
"Kase de battle am in my han'."
Den de lam' ram sheep begin to blow,
Trumpets begin to soun'
Joshua commanded de children to shout
An' de walls come tumblin' down.
Dat mornin'.

    Some rain fell last night, but this happens less and less as the ground bakes, and the rivers die, and the skies stay blue and burning. Everything smells fresh this morning as if the world has just been born, and now the walls go up and no one thinks they will ever tumble down and Berlin is forgotten or remembered differently and no American president is recalled saying take down this wall. No, no, and Jericho is not about murdering and imprisoning people but about freedom and the shuffling of feet in a ring shout and I walk a dirt track at grey light and the agents roll past and they say they work for freedom and I see men sitting on the ground as agents encircle them and all this is also about freedom and the buses roll past with barred windows hauling men and women and children back to the line where the wall stands but their bodies go tumbling down as they are cast back into Mexico and torn from their dreams.

Joshua fit the battle ob Jericho, Jericho, Jericho
Joshua fit de battle ob Jericho
An' de walls come tumblin' down.

Taking Names

There is the matter of anger also. It begins to flow out of me like lava.

For a while, I blamed drink and cut back on my thirst.

Then I said it must be diet and attended to sound nutrition.

Finally, I realized something was happening inside of me, not in some organ, but in that secret place we never have found that we call the soul.

I thought maybe it was Juárez and all those killings.

I thought maybe I have been on bloody ground too long.

I thought and I thought and I no longer believed myself.

I went to New Orleans. I stopped the car and walked to the edge of the swamp and inhaled.

At the café the waitress told me to try the alligator, that it was really good.

I did.

I felt much better.

But the anger remained.

* * *

My old man sits at the maple table in the kitchen with his quart of beer and hand-rolled cigarette. Two loaves of fresh baked bread cool on the rack. The sun fades from the western sky.

He says the stories of Joshua are absurd, that the sun cannot be stilled in the sky since the sun is motionless and the earth orbits around it. He says any God that prolongs a day so that there is more time for killing is beneath contempt. He says only a fool believes such tales and then he takes another swig of beer.

Huddie Ledbetter becomes Lead Belly and he writes the song in between bouts of murder and he is in and out of prisons in Texas and Louisiana and so he knows his walls and in prison one of his regular visitors is a rich white guy named William Edenborn, who made his fortune by manufacturing cheap barbed wire. Lead Belly wound up for a spell doing a hayseed act about how he sang his way out of prison with songs, and in the thirties *Life* magazine put out a story on him called "Bad Nigger Makes Good Minstrel," and he writes that song about taking names.

There's a man going 'round taking names
There's a man going 'round taking names
He's been taking my mother's name
an' he left my heart in vain
there's a man going 'round taking names.

The city burns, the killing goes down, the story, well, it changes and winds up a song about breaking free of chains and walls tumbling down and making it home where there is food and comfort and safety.

And love.

And we'll do a ring shout, yes we will, and the agents will be shuffling counterclockwise, so will the poor men and women and children and Lead Belly, he'll be off to the side strumming his twelve-string guitar and we'll raise up our voices and this will go on for hours and hours outside, down by the creek under the big cottonwood trees and night'll come down and still we'll be singing and shuffling and clapping and we'll say, yes we will, we'll say

Joshua fit the battle ob Jericho, Jericho, Jericho
Joshua fit de battle ob Jericho
An' de walls come tumblin'down.

The Dream

I am dreaming. I am walking down a road, the woman with me is much older and there is spring in the air. The road is dirt and shaded by elms and oaks and apple blossoms smother me with scent. I feel vinegar in my life. In the cellar of an old house sitting on the dirt floor are large crocks with pickles. I am sure of this last, even though I am dreaming, even though I am walking, and my steps take me back to when I was three or four and forward to when I am no more and yet persist as the stones persist and the sunrises and the moon softly splashes on December ground.

On this walk the sun is warm but early, the sun has just begun and the apple blossoms explode with the gift of life as yellow paints the ground and wanders through the green leaves. The woman wears a print dress, has very dark lipstick, a color favored after one of the bigger wars, and her hips swing as the season comes on.

A gray hawk keens nearby—that is how the apple blossoms came back into my life. I walk down another dirt road near the border and a gray hawk screams and suddenly my face is awash with apple blossoms and an older woman, an aunt I suspect, is beside me. A big war has ended and the men have come home and everyone is breeding and the world is open for business and love again. There is vinegar in the air knifing through the blooms and coming from the crocks of pickles in the cellar, but still it is spring as I walk by the creek and suddenly tumble into the past riding the cry of a gray hawk that carries me to apple blossoms and the ground white with petals.

I get up at two a.m. and the stars blaze in a moonless sky.

The band plays "Buffalo Springfield," out under giant pecans along the river. I no longer am in the place where the night feels cool against my skin and the guy beside me tries to smile about the murder of his mother and sister over there across the river, in that place where they live and must be walled off from our world. He is a carpenter fighting for asylum because if he is sent back there he will be killed. There are two fires going—it is that time of night when we all go tribal—there have been hours of food and drink and music and speeches. It is a fundraiser for those who escape with their lives, come north and cross the river and seek shelter. I am under the old pecans in the cool of evening as the band plays and stories hang in the air of murdered and mutilated loved ones and an equation floats in front of me as I look over the crowd.

The man tells me he built doors secretly in a rented house because otherwise they would come and demand money from him.

The man tells me that if the president came to his city without bodyguards he would be murdered within an hour.

He speaks and says I am the last survivor in my family and they dug up the bodies of two brothers and a sister and they burned the family house down and suddenly talk ceases under the big pecan trees.

There was a moment long ago when I drove deep into the north woods to pick up the papers of a retired congressman, the house nestled by a small lake in the cutover region where the Midwest had been gnawed to the ground and the sun was shining that day, the waters a jewel of blue, the house snug but not pretentious and I thought I will work my job, save, and have this place in the woods and every day I will make the earth around me better and every day the earth around me will feed me and I will cease to really exist and become one with something else, melt into a thing of wonder.

This did not happen.

The walls came into my life and on the ground.

Now I am going past the walls.

That is the joy of no-man's-land.

Sandhills overhead in a notched V migrating south from one nation to another and there is no stopping them.

Yes.

I am dreaming.

I have always been dreaming but I did not realize this until I woke up amid the walls and ruined loves.

In the dream, the walls do not tumble down.

In the dream, they never were there at all.

I am dreaming.

Coda

The court, with advice of the elders, ordered a general fast. The occasions were,

1. The ill news we had out of England concerning the breach between the king and parliament.
2. The danger of the Indians.
3. The unseasonable weather, the rain having continued so long, viz., near a fortnight together, scarce one fair day, and much corn and hay spoiled, though indeed it proved a blessing to us, for it being with warm easterly winds, it brought the Indian corn to maturity, which otherwise would not have been ripe, and it pleased God, that so soon as the fast was agreed upon, the weather changed, and proved fair after.

Much disputation there was about liberty of removing for outward advantages, and all ways were sought for an open door to get out at; but it is to be feared many crept out at a broken wall. For such as come together into a wilderness, where are nothing but wild beasts and beastlike men, and there confederate together in civil and church estate, whereby they do, implicitly at least, bind themselves to support each other, and all of them that society, whether civil or sacred, whereof they are members. How they can break from this without free consent is hard to find, so as may satisfy a tender or good conscience in time of trial. Ask thy conscience, if thou wouldst have plucked up thy stakes, and brought thy family 3,000 miles, if thou hadst expected that all, or most, would have forsaken thee there. Ask again, what liberty thou hast towards others, which thou likest not to allow others towards thyself, for if one may go, another may, and so the greater part, and so church and common-wealth may be left destitute in a wilderness, exposed to misery and reproach, and all for thy ease and pleasure, whereas these all, being now thy brethren, as near to thee as the Israelites were to Moses, it were much safer for thee, after his example, to choose rather to suffer affliction with thy brethren, than to enlarge thy ease and pleasure by furthering the occasion of their ruin.

John Winthrop, governor of the Massachusetts Bay Colony, in his journal, dated September 22, 1642, on the endless fear gnawing at the entrails of the City on a Hill

Below me are the lights of the town,
like a ship that can never depart.

J. A. BAKER, *The Hill of Summer*

Notes

7   *And he says, "I am not going*: Taylor Branch, *Pillar of Fire: America in the King Years, 1963–65* (New York: Simon & Schuster, 1998), 514.

22   *In 1964, when Lyndon Johnson*: Branch, *Pillar of Fire*, 299.

27   *As he explained to Frank Lansing*: Pankaj Mishra, "Watch this man," *London Review of Books* 33, no. 21 (November 3, 2011), lrb.co.uk/v33/n21/pankaj-mishra/watch-this-man.

33   *Later she says*: Lynn Brezosky, "Family: Not leaving without David," October 11, 2010, mysanantonio.com/news/mexico/article/Family -Not-leaving-without-David-697789.php.

33   *Tiffany Hartley cannot describe the attackers*: "Borderline Madness: Falcon Lake Murder," youtube.com/watch?v=jWL2f_jyLJ4& feature=related.

55   *I know my way is rough and steep*: From "The Wayfaring Stranger," a traditional folk song originating in the early nineteenth century.

58   *I'm going there to see my mother*: From "The Wayfaring Stranger."

59   *I want to wear a crown of glory*: From "The Wayfaring Stranger."

65   *For ten years or more*: Alan Gomez, Jack Gillum, and Kevin Johnson, "U.S. border cities prove havens from Mexico's drug violence," *USA Today*, July 18, 2011, usatoday.com/news/washington/2011-07-15 -border-violence-main_n.htm#; Kristin M. Finklea, "Southwest Border Violence: Issues in Identifying and Measuring Spillover Violence," Congressional Research Service Report for Congress, 7-5700, February 28, 2013, fas.org/sgp/crs/homesec/R41075.pdf.

66   *Governor Rick Perry of Texas says*: Eric Lach, "Gov. Perry: Those Who Doubt Tiffany Hartley's Lake Pirates Story 'Ought to Be

Ashamed,'" Talking Points Memo, October 6, 2010, tpmmuckraker
.talkingpointsmemo.com/2010/10/gov_perry_those_who_doubt
_tiffany_hartleys_story_a.php.

66   *Sheriff Sigifredo Gonzalez Jr. of Zapata County*: "Border sheriff
      warns: We're overwhelmed," *WorldNetDaily*, November 12, 2005,
      wnd.com/2005/11/33381.

69   *Tiffany Hartley said she and her husband knew of the robberies*:
      Eric Lach, "Wife of 'Lake Pirates' Victim Speaks Out as Mexican
      Authorities Question Story," Talking Points Memo, October 5, 2010,
      tpmmuckraker.talkingpointsmemo.com/2010/10/wife_of_lake
      _pirates_victim_speaks_out.php#more.

69   *In March two reporters were kidnapped*: "Drug-related violence
      endangers media in Reynosa," Committee to Protect Journalists,
      March 11, 2010, cpj.org/2010/03/drug-related-violence-endangers
      -media-in-reynosa.php.

69   *During a three-week period in February*: Jo Tuckman and Ed
      Vulliamy, "Mexico's drug wars rage out of control," *Guardian*,
      March 23, 2010, guardian.co.uk/world/2010/mar/23/mexico-drug
      -wars-cartels.

70   *By fall, a leader of the ruling party*: Jason Beaubien, "Mexico's
      Reynosa Sees Surge In Violence," GPB Media, October 15, 2010,
      gpb.org/news/2010/10/16/mexicos-reynosa-sees-surge-in
      -violence.

91   *All this is in the House report*: John R. Carter, Republican Confer-
      ence Secretary, "Broken Neighbor, Broken Border," A Field Investi-
      gation Report of the House Immigration Reform Caucus, US House
      of Representatives, November 19, 2010, 9–10, carter.house.gov
      /uploads/Broken-Neighbor-Broken-Border.pdf.

102   *Improvisations that went like this*: Taylor Branch, *At Canaan's
      Edge: America in the King Years, 1965–1968* (New York: Simon &
      Schuster, 2006), 84.

104   *Aldo Leopold made a stab*: Aldo Leopold, *Marshland Elegy* (Madi-
      son: Wisconsin Center for the Book, 1999, originally published in
      A Sand Country Almanac, 1949).

131   *Moses tells the people they have a choice*: Deut. 30:19.

144   *POLICE INVESTIGATE CITY'S LATEST HOMICIDE*: *El Paso Times*,
      Saturday, May 16, 2009.

150   *He is very protective of his people*: Actually a former cartel member
      but I want to cloud his identity.

151   *But nothing is ever stable*: James C. McKinley Jr., "Mexico Drug War Causes Wild West Blood Bath," *New York Times*, April 16, 2008, nytimes.com/2008/04/16/world/americas/16mexico.html.

188   *Try with your pencils*: Carl Sandburg, "Halstead Street Car," *Chicago Poems* (New York: Henry Holt & Co., 1916).

190   *I WANTED a man's face*: Sandburg, "Aztec Mask," *Chicago Poems*.

197   *In 1840, on a hunt*: John James Audubon, *Ornithological Biography, or An Account of the Habits of the Birds of the United States of America* (Edinburgh: Adam Black, 1831–1839), Vol. 3, 204.

197   *J. W. Preston found a nest of a whooping crane*: Jeffrey Moussaieff Masson and Susan McCarthy, *When Elephants Weep: The Emotional Lives of Animals* (New York: Delacorte Press, 1995), 12.

198   *Claude Eagleson remembers*: Gay M. Gomez, "Whooping Cranes in Southwest Louisiana: History and Human Attitudes," in D. W. Stahlecker, ed., *Proceedings of the Sixth North American Crane Workshop, Oct. 3–5, 1991, Regina, Sask.* (Grand Island, NE: North American Crane Working Group, 1992), 19–23, digitalcommons .unl.edu/nacwgproc/262.

200   *It can only be achieved when men and women*: Martin Luther King's "Beyond Vietnam" address, given at New York City's Riverside Church on April 4, 1967.

201   *It is the fall of 1967*: Hampton Sides, *Hellhound on His Trail: The Stalking of Martin Luther King, Jr. and the International Hunt for his Assassin* (New York: Doubleday, 2010), 25–33.

203   *The families of the dead men lack the money*: Sides, *Hellhound on His Trail*, 77–78.

204   *I may not get there with you*: Martin Luther King Jr., "I've Been to the Mountaintop," April 3, 1968.

ABOUT THE AUTHOR

Author of many acclaimed books about the American Southwest and US-Mexico border issues, CHARLES BOWDEN (1945–2014) was a contributing editor for *GQ*, *Harper's*, *Esquire*, and *Mother Jones* and also wrote for the *New York Times Book Review*, *High Country News*, and *Aperture*. His honors included a PEN First Amendment Award, the Lannan Literary Award for Nonfiction, and the Sidney Hillman Award for outstanding journalism that fosters social and economic justice.

ABOUT THE AUTHOR OF THE FOREWORD

CHARLES D'AMBROSIO is the author of two books of fiction, *The Point and Other Stories*, a finalist for the PEN/Hemingway Award, and *The Dead Fish Museum*, a finalist for the PEN/Faulkner Award. He is also the author of two collections of essays, *Orphans*, and *Loitering: New & Collected Essays*. Many of his stories originally appeared in *The New Yorker*, and he has also published fiction in *The Paris Review*, *Zoetrope All-Story*, and *A Public Space*. His work has been widely anthologized and selected for the Pushcart Prize, *Best American Short Stories*, and the O. Henry Award. He has been the recipient of a Lannan Literary Fellowship, a Whiting Writer's Award, and an Academy Award in Literature from the American Academy of Arts and Letters. He teaches fiction at the Iowa Writers' Workshop.